ART & DESIGN

ACADEMY GROUP LTD
42 LEINSTER GARDENS, LONDON W2 3AN
TEL: 071-402 2141 FAX: 071-723 9540

EDITOR: Nicola Kearton
SUB-EDITOR: Stephen Watt
ART EDITOR: Andrea Bettella
CHIEF DESIGNER: Mario Bettella
DESIGNERS: Toby Norman, Phil Kirwin

SUBSCRIPTION OFFICES:
UK: VCH PUBLISHERS (UK) LTD
8 WELLINGTON COURT, WELLINGTON STREET
CAMBRIDGE CB1 1HZ
TEL: (0223) 321111 FAX: (0223) 313321

USA AND CANADA: VCH PUBLISHERS INC
303 NW 12TH AVENUE DEERFIELD BEACH,
FLORIDA 33442-1788 USA
TEL: (305) 428-5566 / (800) 367-8249
FAX: (305) 428-8201

ALL OTHER COUNTRIES:
VCH VERLAGSGESELLSCHAFT MBH
BOSCHSTRASSE 12, POSTFACH 101161
69451 WEINHEIM
FEDERAL REPUBLIC OF GERMANY
TEL: 06201 606 148 FAX: 06201 606 184

CONTENTS

*Glenn Brown, Dali-Christ,
1992, oil, 275x183cm, see
pp6-19 (Karsten Schubert,
London)*

*Virgil Tracy, The Apotheosis
of . . ., 1994, see ppII-V*

*Leonora Robinson,
Untitled, 1994, see pp68-75*

STARS IN YOUR EYES

FOOTBALL AND VIRGIL TRACY

Joanne Hill

'The metaphorical richness of sport is so inextricably bound up with English society, a persuasive microcosm of the encoded nature of social distinctions, aspirations and mores. Add to this the bookmakers and we have a perfect analogy of market capitalism.' Mark Wallinger

'Five days shalt thou labour, as the Bible says. The seventh day is the Lord thy God's. The sixth day is for football and spreading the word and punishing and suchlike.' Anthony Burgess

Why has Sport become so fashionable? Why does it dominate mainstream culture? To paraphrase Robert Hughes in *The Culture of Complaint*, sport like art, is an arena in which elitism can display itself at a negligible cost in social harm. Historians and social anthropologists argue that you can't study social change without examining the pornography peculiar to that era. The same must apply, certainly in this century, to football which has come bounding out of the cultural closet to find its feet on the dance floor, in theatre/ opera and on the Art scene.

Jan Hoet's 1992 Kassel Documenta was a self-styled 'Olympics of art', including sport/art crossovers such as soccer goals with stained-glass windows instead of nets (Wim Delvoye); pastiche Maleviches painted in the colours of Premiership sides (Keith Coventry) and videos with protagonists in American football gear (Matthew Barney).

It's not just artists who have become convinced of the potential of football, but writers and politicians too. Advertisers are just as fond of using football personalities – Keegan and Brut, Charlton and Shredded Wheat, Clough and East Midlands Electric, Gary *Welcome Home* Lineker Walkers Crisps – as politicians are of football metaphors – Douglas Hurd is a safe pair of hands; Michael Heseltine isn't a team player; at Warrington, the IRA scored an own goal. *Granta* and *The London Review of Books* waxed lyrical over Gazza while the Tories lumped sports and arts together in one ministry; an unholy alliance offering little more than David Chelsea strip Mellor as the six-o-six show host.

Anyone looking for a handy, lazy symbol of our post-war decline can always rely on our international side to provide it. You need a weak and feeble football manager to dramatise the plight of a weak and feeble PM? No problem. *Nick Hornby*
The language of both politicians and advertisers is, for the very reason that they are both interested only in pure persuasion, by the easiest rhetorical means to hand – the language a culture uses when it has dropped its guard and has been caught simply chatting to itself. The liturgy is unmistakable and slightly dispiriting. Altogether, now: 'Ooh! Ah! Can-to-na . . .', 'Let's all do the Merson . . .' 'Big fat Ron's barmy army!' *Tom Shone,* The Sunday Times, *May 29th 1994*

However, artist Virgil Tracy, in a series of redemptive works relating to football, fans and fame seeks to redress this balance of media appropriation; the fan strikes back, chanting enigmatically from the terraces: 'Virgil Tracy there's only one Virgil Tracy'. Agency and dignity are restored to transference and projection. We enter as if by osmosis a looking-glass world of simple, instantly legible archetypes and characters: our own, where play rules the day and we are free to indulge and rehearse our desires; to probe the relationship between psyche and wannabe – a stars in your eyes twilight zone.

At the centre of the conceptual artist's work is the refusal to separate Art from Life. The emphasis is placed squarely on the 'idea' and the desire to reverse the split between creator and consumer, for art to be democratised, assimilated and dispensed throughout society. The work manifests itself not from traditional media and materials but from such sources as language, sociology, politics and popular culture.

Virgil Tracy seems intent on collapsing the whole social edifice, he lives his life as a series of performances, often using surveillance media and theory-based reportage to interrogate the subtle erosion of civil liberties. His instinct for revealing detail and moderate style often threatens to implode but the viewer is too implicated to take issue with him for looking in the first place. He has achieved some notoriety, not least through his name. Christened David Owen, but fed up with jokes about the SDP leader, he changed his name by deed poll to his favourite *Thunderbirds* character. Having discovered how easy a legal process it was, he developed a taste for it. In a gesture of solidarity with a 71-year-old poll tax defaulter who was imprisoned for 23 days, he changed his name to William 'Des' Atkinson. This evolved into *Identikit* a performance piece for the 1993 Sheffield Media show. Masquerading as gallery 'security' he exhibited some personal ephemera, his birth certificate and baby photos. As audience members arrived, they had to sign themselves in; by the time they left, they discovered that the attendant-artist had changed his name to their name and displayed the legal document on the wall for all to see. During the course of a week he changed his name 82 times.

Index (Now 93, Nottingham) focused attention on the data we impart for storage on file. This official but partial documentation becomes our legal, fixed characterisation. The unwitting subject queued in a disused court building; volunteering information including thermal photographs (via CCTV), signatures and fingerprints. The evidence was eventually shredded and returned; ensuring that it could not be viewed out of context.

Device and A Public Bugging questioned the use of surveillance techniques in modern shopping complexes and on the street to undermine privacy in public spaces.

A Good Book (Locus + 1994) is a version of the Bible which complicates our assumptions about freedom of speech. On one level it is simply a series of impressive recordings; transcribed and elegantly framed. These chart the grotesque cadences of Nottingham evangelists; obtrusive figures who exert a fascination. Their style and content is direct and discriminatory, nobody is exempt from their cautionary sermonising: Jews, gays, women, pop stars, all other creeds and cultures. Text-based artwork demands the active participation of readers who must concentrate on the extraordinary physical exchange that exists, in this case, between themselves and the preachers – a dubious privilege indeed.

Tracy reinstates the challenge of dialogue at the centre of his Work, rather than trying to reach any kind of categorical agreement; offering drama without catharsis, confrontation without resolution, and provocation without redress. On occasion the expression of this work can seem so perfunctory as to render normal artistic judgement perverse, helping to push away from Art and back to Life. He simplifies and purifies his forms, ridding them of excrescences. He opines that less 'intervention' is more; preserving things in motion and then letting them alone, resisting absolute control to allow them to take their course and their chances. Many works are dependent on a direct interaction between artist and public for their evolution. Whimsy, polemic and attitude inhabit the same space. The sacralisation of objects of an ordinary (very British ordinary) kind is considered. He is the Philip Larkin of conceptual art – without the wanking.

Back to football. The primary skills of association football involve the ability to play with a ball. In simple terms, the outfield players have to be able to control the ball and direct passes and shots at goal effectively. So what's the big deal? Every one has a stake in the game. Supporters want good facilities at low prices and to see their own team win. Clubs covet more income from television and bigger wealthier crowds. Players seek higher wages and fewer games. Television demands more live games at the convenience of advertisers. The blissfully cruel irony is that all these diverse interests depend utterly on each other, forced into unhappy relationships that continue in more or less permanent public rows.

The British game has always been about passion and characters who get into trouble. Take all those characters away and I don't think people would be really bothered about going to watch games. *Vinny Jones* Football is a casualty of the circulation war between Murdoch & Maxwell . . . Racing is a stone cold certainty compared to football. Horses don't have women problems or agents, don't fall out with the outside-right and refuse to give him the ball and don't demand pay rises. *Ken Bates Chelsea Chairman*

The banishment of Diego Maradona and the murder of Andreas Escobar suddenly put the competition back in touch with football as the rest of the world knows it – a simple game that has become an obsession with poor and rich alike. For all the stylistic and commercial differences, the essentials of football are the same around the world. For its characters, the personal dividend of a life in football may be profit, or political power, or merely some form of personal revenge.

Three appalling events: Heysel, Hillsborough and Bradford gave birth to more fanzines, the Taylor report and ultimately, a more positive government approach to football. Fans are bound together by a mutual fascination with a game which despite all its casualties and tragedies – its Gascoignes, Grobbelaars, Shiltons and Cantonas – carries a special resonance. If English football may be in a terrible state on the pitch – its cultural away-days would seem to be on top form. There may be some connection between the two. In the recent anthology *My Favourite Year*, edited by Nick Hornby, Ed Horton writes: 'There is a paradox in football's literature: the closer you get to the game itself, the less compelling your narrative becomes.'

Novels about sport are always problematic. The actual game comes across as faintly unreal. Off the pitch there is far more drama. Nick Hornby's achievement in *Fever Pitch* was to have circumvented this problem completely by instead anatomising the obsessive pathology of the fan – not so much on the head as in it, perhaps – and thereby to have addressed the subject of men's feelings in much the same way that feminist texts

Studies for A Soccer Skills Wallchart, *1994*

did women's in the 1970s.

I like playing football because I can play with my friends, Rhianna, Richard, Jamie and Adrian, and it's good exercise. I get so excited when I'm kicking the ball. I'm good at tackling and scoring. I go to practise with the school team but I won't be in it because I don't like the kit. I've never been to a proper match but I watch them on TV. I hate Liverpool. I'd like to be Ryan Giggs or Peter Schmeichel but I don't fancy them. *Daisy Ruth Rands, superstriker, age 10*

Do narcissistic yearnings mask a licensed homoerotic public orgy, central to modern masculinity's inherent fraudulence? A common misconception about football is that it has always been the sanctum sanctorium of British maleness. Maybe pictures speak louder than words. Tracy's *Soccer Skills Wallchart* expands upon emotional themes without being gender specific; becoming more coercive for making proximity to the game the point. He dispels a few myths:

I'm really irritated by people who talk about male supporters as if they are all football hooligans. I also reject the 'feminist free zone argument', girls have aspirational fantasies too and lots of them are football fans. In a crowd there's an unambiguous display of comradeship and belief. I equate football with success on a personal level and with unleashing emotions and particularly restoring a sense of authenticity to general perceptions of emotions.

I can appreciate this. In my pre-teen years I wore the coveted George Best no 11 strip and had fantasies about being Gerry Daly/both Brian and Jimmy Greenhoff/Willie Morgan and Lou Macari. I once cried, really sobbed, over United's FA Cup defeat in 1976, hastily drafting a tearstained letter of support to Tommy Docherty and the boys; today, amongst my peers, I'd be hailed as some sort of grand diva of the ironic gesture. But I wouldn't enjoy that half as much as I'd enjoyed crying.

Having established that he's no Iron John I have to question the ego thing which is heavily foregrounded. Is Tracy in crisis? Is he a collapsing new man? Is he just being indulgent?

Yes to all of those. Of course I am indulgent. I've invested a lot of time in this. The ego thing is a big deal. By making works such as *The Apotheosis of* . . . and the *Soccer Skills Wallchart*, I am realising a dream, and though there is no active participation in the game, I am reaping the benefits; idolisation being one of them. The completed Wallchart will be sent to the 92 Premiership and Football League managers, requesting a trial for the club concerned. In the unlikely event of one of these requests being accepted, the trial will form part of a video package. What is more important is

that 92 clubs will be made aware of my existence as a footballer. The idea of actually playing the game really terrifies me. I do not have and have never had what it takes to turn professional. I come from a background where I lived and breathed football. I was taken to watch Blackpool at the age of seven and have been going ever since. It's like a sort of madness in which I am compelled to attend every game, no matter how insignificant. For two hours every Saturday, I become a part of something and display all the characteristics commonly attributed to football supporters.

The surface subjectivity, a feature that might raise a cavil or two elsewhere, is more celebratory than sentimental and is crucial to an understanding of the relationship between the fan and their idealised projection. Dreams become goals in your very own fantasy football league. This seductive conceptual key invites viewers to consider their complicity with the big themes of transference and solipsism as personal and social narratives merge. Tracy explains:

You can be both a heroic individual and part of a crowd at the same time. Sometimes I stand alone so that I can immerse myself totally, in the atmosphere and in the game itself. It's the only time that I really lose myself and it constantly surprises me that it is in something so trivial as a game.

These Works originate in the idea of replacing the gallery with a stadium as the ultimate venue for an artwork. A desire to establish a new audience led to *The Apotheosis of* . . . during the first part of 1994. The scoreboard piece demonstrated the fact that the terrace throng relive their fantasy about playing for a club at a professional level; you might say that supporters are potential players who aren't good enough. Most fans dream of running out of the tunnel with their favourite team while the fans call out their name – this was the silent version – using LED boards at matches. Few artists can say 186,000 viewers saw their work, in this case 'One Virgil Tracy. There's only one Virgil Tracy'; flashed across electronic scoreboards at Premier League games all over the country. Yet a fascination with football, fans and fame might be seen as a departure from earlier, more overtly political work?

I love to question my obsession – the fan and fame part of the question – with football, particularly Blackpool FC; I can only support a lower division club. So it's a regional and therefore political investment too. It's not about watching quality football, if it was I'd go to Manchester United or Blackburn Rovers. Maybe that's a very British characteristic – an unexplainable passion for something which has few merits like lower division football. In *Fever Pitch*, Nick Hornby painted an accurate portrait of the life of a football supporter.

However there is a problem with the way he views the game. Travelling to dreary towns like Hartlepool in the middle of winter is a vital part of the existence of lower league soccer, and with all due respect to Nick Hornby, he hasn't had to make such journeys very often. He supports Arsenal – a team from the south, Tracy visibly shudders,

and his accounts are littered with complaints about them not winning a trophy for five years or so. In the 23 years I have been watching Blackpool, I have witnessed the following successes; promotion from the 4th to the 3rd division in 1985 and promotion from the 4th to the 3rd division via the Wembley play-offs in 1992.

Tracy's amusing interactive colour-in wallchart was designed to counteract the Ryan Giggs soccer skills TV programme. Shirts, shorts and socks are blank outlines, as Tracy designs himself out of the text, to be filled in according to the viewer's choice of escapist drag:

I had to shoot a couple of rolls of film to get enough usable shots. I am anonymous apart from the credit 'soccer skills demonstrated by Virgil Tracy' and a printed autograph – obviously.

A nostalgia for the halcyon, pre-greed days of the game is reflected in the choice of solid blocks of colour: green, fleshtone and black, the primitive graphic style of 60s and 70s instruction manuals. The sequence of striker poses in the illustrations: traps, headers, volleys, tackles, shots, overhead kicks and passes resemble Action Hero transfers carefully stencilled onto painted turf backgrounds; an echo of the fans' transference of their desires onto the players.

Many of the new artists – bar Wallinger – don't want to politicise sport, if anything they want to let it be. Perhaps reducing it to a primitive and mostly proletarian culture which the artist-anthropologist can effortlessly patronise? The game's ludicrous aura of solemnity is tinged with a deeply ingrained proletarian snobbery (football and 'masculinity' in Britain, like everything else, become class issues). In Koon's terms, sport is 'pre-birth', so even someone with only one brain cell can feel superior. Since the end of the Cold War sport has been relatively de-politicised. For the first time since the 30s, male intellectuals of the left are misty-eyed over the Olympics and the World Cup. For some, sport is a beautiful ballsy oasis in an ugly, emasculated world. Body of Cruyff. Amen.

As a British artist, I find myself needing to make works about subjects which are culturally significant to the country I live in or subjects I understand. Football unites the two and I see myself making football related works for quite some time. I'm working on a piece at the moment using replica shirts. The replica shirt business is quite a recent phenomena and has become a huge industry, but I feel that clubs like Manchester United have taken unfair advantage of their supporters, I challenge them to justify the need for four different kits.

Commerce has definitely taken over, it's becoming a middle class game sanctioned by cultural critics, the unemployed are being priced out of matches. It's about lower division clubs, always the backbone of British football providing great players who came through the ranks, now having to sell their best players in order to survive, about how the game has become ruled by money and greed. In that sense we're back with the previous question, this work is as political as some of the surveillance pieces and I can draw a continuity out of my artistic evolution.

Virgil Tracy, A Good Book, *was published by Locus+, Newcastle-upon-Tyne, 1994*

The Apotheosis of . . ., *1994*

CONSTELLATIONS
Michael Petry

David Thorpe (Director, South London Gallery) wanted to exhibit Shaheen Merali's *Channels, Echoes and Empty Chairs* and my *The Garden of Enlightenment*, together for a variety of reasons; the show was called 'Constellations'. The most obvious reason was that they both employ interactive elements. Merali places sound beams in the space that released tonal information when activated by the viewers. People were encouraged physically to enter my work and gather up the fibre optic cables to form an image. Both works use high tech materials in unexpected ways. The sound beams were developed for dance performances, and the cables are those being laid across the world as part of the digital information highway.

We are interested in how information is used, gathered and controlled. Merali looks at issues of race and sexism and how stereotyped images of non-Western peoples have been used, while my subversively beautiful cables allude to an ever increasing ability to keep tabs on citizens under the seductive guise of protection. Merali has collected over 700 objects and 5,000 postcards depicting 'Third World people' in racially questionable ways. We both control the images and amount of information the viewer gets at any one time and in the Information Age, those who control this have real power. My concern about censorship was brought to life when the local Labour council sent down an officer to preview the work. It was rumoured that the video was pornographic, depicting two men engaged in coitus and masturbation and in contravention of the infamous Clause 28. As the video did not depict such acts, nor ever allow the viewer to know the sex of the lover of the male actor (Michael Cashman: actor and well known gay rights activist), the work could not be censored. Their action only served to highlight the inbuilt homophobia (and general prejudice) of society, its monitoring, and attempts at the controlling of non-status quo ideas reaching the general public. Whether racist, homophobic or merely non partisan, all information, public and increasingly private, is under the watchful eye of the state, and technological advances place it at their fingertips for whatever use. Merali and I are interested in questioning those who would control information for 'the public good'.

The content of both works is based on a system

of viewing the universe, Merali's on Astrology, mine on Astronomy. Merali's work is composed of many parts that coalesce into a coherent installation that is a whole, in mine, the fibre optics take the whole video and disperse it pixel by pixel into individual dots of light, impossible to be seen as a whole, other than as a work. Merali used texts by Professor Douglas Smith charting the astrological state when Merali purchased the trinkets. Merali had documented the dates and times in order for Smith to draw up charts (painted on the walls) which described how Merali must have felt based on the stars. These texts can be read as humorous or serious, but placed on the floor (behind glass), they encouraged viewers to stoop to read, thus setting off the sound. My video character contrasts the feelings and knowledge of the state of his sexual relationship with cosmological events (black holes, super string theory), and the impossibility of objective truth. The sex of the lover is hidden from the viewer, first by a sheet and then by language: Cashman speaks only of 'my lover' or to 'you'. The withholding of information parallels the impossibility of total enlightenment. Further meaning came from knowing Cashman's sexuality; it prejudices the viewer's concept of whether the video lover was male or female. Cashman may be a gay man, but is not a gay actor.

Merali used computers (Adobe Photoshop) to merge the dubious collectibles with images made in the studio and his soundscape was created with composer Philip Chambon. Gavin Greenaway and John Powell, my long term collaborators, wrote the invaluable *Garden* soundtrack. Merali's works have focused on projections and the nature of the projected image. Meaning within the image, subject and pictorial content refers to historically hidden subtexts. He explores post modernity and post-colonialism, through the rewriting of history and returns the Western gaze with a view from the East. A self-conscious view of his own history parallels that of a body politic, bodies as subtext. Merali has stated that he wants to tune into his emotions about situations about tensions new to global society. He finds links between the Indian Independence Movement and troubles in East London. Merali looks for patterns that re-emerge, and uses his body as a starting point. *Channels, Echoes and Empty Chairs* was an open-ended project, unique in his practice. Made over a two year period, the collection of people, images, and sounds, formed an ongoing interactive dialogue. Merali collaborates on his installations requiring of others musical or computer skills, but in this work the individual's presence and reactive pose was what was most desired. Musical interventions by Aniruddha Das (Asian Dub Foundation) have acted as dialogues for performance as in *Going*

Native (Bluecoat, Arnolfini and Ikon Galleries). Merali created a scenario where the audience interacted with the video as they walked through the projection beam. The music, strands of classical Western music was disrupted by classical Asian sounds. Merali makes people feel comfortable with their stereotypes, only to disrupt them by juxtaposing the 'other'. A *Channels* image of Barbie wearing a sari was merged with a real Asian 'untouchable' woman. Barbie is worth more than the woman could earn in a year. Similar images in the same picture plane, but an exclusivity of goods and worlds . The 'untouchable' woman cannot touch Barbie because of the cost, and Barbie is 'untouchable' for Merali because of what she embodies.

In works like *The Chemistry of Love*, or *Flight from Technology* I have explored the relationship between science and art. Seductive materials, technologically advanced or not like silk, cotton, laboratory glass or fibre optic cable are infused with video links that bind the erotic to the scientific. These works suggest that ration and emotion are two sides of the same coin that meet somewhere in the middle. I use video as a source of light and information, deconstructed its materiality to light emission merges form and content. In *The Garden,* video was present in its essence as light. The fibre ends provided a measure of information, yet the rest, scattered around the viewer, while accessible to some extent, was beyond reach. David Thorpe asked if it was possible to create a video work seen in daylight, so often they are in dark rooms. The mixture of natural and artificial light was a major consideration. The soundtrack (emanating from hidden speakers in the wall) added to the frustrated desire to 'see' the video in a traditional sense, as it engaged the viewer in the world of the speaker. The introduction of a narrative line was a significant break in my practice that came from working with the actor Mark Rylance on my previous video installation, *The Blizzard*. Rylance played Buzz, whose life is disrupted by technological failures, and while narrative in structure, owed more to an earlier *faux* documentary style. The video for *The Garden* was made to be seen in parallel as separate works. The video was made to be seen in broadcast, as well as being an integral part of the installation. Viewers entered a long narrow hall from outside and could see in the distance what appeared to be a small room with a low black ceiling. Only upon entering the room, did the scale explode into view. This was the first indication that everything was not what it appeared to be. Structurally, visually, as well as in the video content, *The Garden of Enlightenment* is a paradigm shift in my production; not surprising given the title.

'Constellations', South London Gallery 1994, pages VI-VII: Michael Petry, The Garden of Enlightenment, *photos Edward Woodman; OPPOSITE and ABOVE: Shaheen Merali,* Channels, Echoes and Empty Chairs

BOOK WORKS

Peggy Rawes

B ased in London, Book Works was set up in 1985 to promote and publish artists' books as well as a variety of text-based projects. Rather than focusing on the craft-based or the illustrative traditions of artists' books, Book Works commissions interdisciplinary projects with artists which more closely relate to the contemporary visual arts, especially conceptual, time-based or installation work.

Each book represents an exploration both into the conceptual nature of its own subject matter and further into the scope of what a book itself may be. The physical character of the book, its dimensions, weight, choice of ink, paper, typography, format and sequence of 'narrative', are therefore often as important to the meaning of the book as the subject matter. As a result, the reader may also be given a more pronounced role in determining how to interpret the book's contents; just as time-based and installation works encourage the spectator to participate actively in their interpretation.

The following books explore a number of the particular concerns which Book Works is keen to promote and present in their collaboration with artists who use text in their visual work. For the artists, the opportunity allows them to develop their ideas in a new context. *Coloured People* (1987) and *My Book The East London Coelacanth* (1993) explore the relationship between language, history and culture and race. *Notable Days* (1990) and *The Price of Words* (1992) reflect concerns about historical and political events in Europe and Jewish identity, respectively. *The Stumbling Block, Its Index*, (1990) *Two Oxford Reading Rooms* (1994) and *Rex Reason* (1994) consider the physical character of text and different systems of thought (a scientific chart, a university library, a fictional narrative) which closely relate to contemporary artistic practice. *Lost Volumes, A Catalogue of Disasters* (1993) plays with the illusionistic properties of the photograph and the printed page and, most recently, *J'appelle un chat un chat* (1994) considers how Freud's psychoanalysis of hysteria can be read as a framework in the construction of female identity and language.

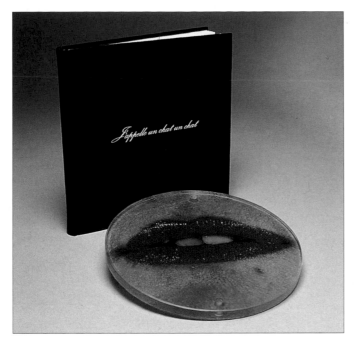

J'appelle un chat un chat by Sharon Kivland, published in an edition of 10 copies, each signed by the artist, and hand printed and bound at Book Works.

This is the second artist's book to be produced by American artist Kivland in conjunction with Book Works, and has also been shown in the exhibition of the same name at YYZ Toronto, Canada and at Centre d'Arts Plastiques de Saint-Fons, France. The book incorporates text and photographs (each copy has a unique framed photograph on the front) and presents a contemporary response to an extract from Sigmund Freud's psychoanalysis of hysteria in the *Case Histories of Dora*. Kivland uses Freud's slippage into euphemism to describe the female body and sexuality as a starting point for examining constructions of female identity and language. The book is comprised of photographs of women wearing different shades of lipstick accompanied by words which both describe the names of red lipsticks and can be understood as descriptions of different emotional states. As a result it provides a critical commentary on Freud's use of language within a scientific study and also invites the reader to examine the relationship between images of women, psychoanalysis and language in a contemporary context.

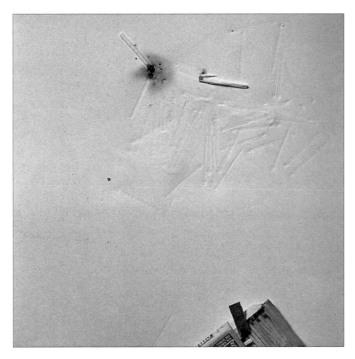

Lost Volume: A Catalogue of Disasters by Cornelia Parker, photography by Edward Woodman, printed offset, 32pp, soft cover.

This sequence of 13 black and white double-spread photographs shows the effect of crushing or flattening domestic objects between two sheets of paper. The book's subsequent contents pages present the 13 objects in orderly, framed illustrations and show five more whole objects which do not appear crushed in the previous pages. (It appears that disaster in this context can mean both damage to objects and their loss.) As a result, these contents pages introduce the transformation of the objects from whole and familiar items into new distorted or unrecognisable forms.

Rather than just invoking ideas of loss or nostalgia, British artist Cornelia Parker suggests new appreciation of the materials and form of objects which have undergone dramatic change. Each photograph re-emphasises the idea that the objects can represent a momento mori. It could be said that each image contains a 'death' through the loss of the object's original function.

In addition, Edward Woodman's photography and the indentation each object has made, seemingly on the page opposite, contribute to the effect of the transformation of the original three-dimensional object into a two-dimensional still life.

My Book, The East London Coelacanth, Sometimes Called, Troubled Waters; The Story of British Sea-Power by Jimmie Durham, ICA/Book Works, black & White ills, 48pp, hard-backed.

As the length of this book's title suggests, Durham does not always like to follow the rules of literary convention.

Through a visual narrative and accompanying writing, Durham (artist and native American Indian) amuses, frustrates and seduces the reader into the fictional tale of the search for this historical fish said to live in the Thames. It is a story of cultural, professional and personal experience of identity, and it gently interrogates Western attitudes towards otherness, the primitive and, through the metaphor of the Coelacanth, the potential of extinction. During this journey Durham also asks teasing questions about authorship, classification and the art market which reflect the wit and acumen of his performance and visual work.

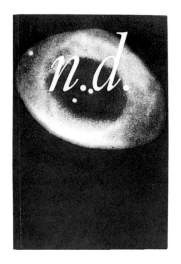 

Notable Days by Pavel Büchler, offset litho, black & white & colour, 208pp, soft cover.

One of the aims of Büchler's book is to bring together a range of ideas about how we receive and consume visual and written information. Photographs taken from the media and a sequence of dates, which do not have the year marked, present a chronology of connections which require the reader to take a range of approaches in order to decipher their meaning.

Büchler, a Czech living in Britain, illustrates the degree to which images and dates can be removed or dislocated from their specific historical significance to have little of their original intended meaning left. Specifically, Büchler suggests how the events surrounding November 1989 and the end of totalitarian control in his native Prague can be seen as distant and fractured experiences. Images of banners and crowds appear as abstract tones and shapes. By the use of expanded newsprint throughout the book, Büchler suggests that there is a contradiction between the passing of time and the 20th century's reliance on the visual evidence of events.

The Stumbling Block, Its Index by Brian Catling, case bound with hand-worked graphite boards and embossed title.

This book presents a sequence of poetic passages which explore the 'shape-shifting' nature of a fictional concept, the Stumbling Block. British artist Brian Catling observes how the Stumbling Block is present in artistic, cultural, linguistic and historical contexts. It may occur in the form of a book being used as a doorstop, a typographic font, a nightmare or a rock in a desert.

Drawing upon the styles of religious, meditative and poetic verse, Catling indicates the possible materials and thoughts which may make up the Stumbling Block. For example, he begins, 'The Stumbling Block is a graphite font. This black plinth was once a brush or similar terminal that was the lips of an intense electrical arc.' This passage immediately reminds the reader of the book's own graphite covers and embossed title and reflects the materials and processes which are part of creating objects, ideas and art which Catling explores in both this book and in his performances.

Like the act of contemplating a work of art this book requires moments of absorption in and reflection on the different forms in which the Stumbling Block may exist.

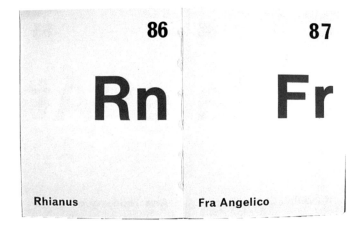

Rex Reason by Simon Patterson, printed offset litho, 116 pp, soft cover.

British artist Simon Patterson has dedicated each page of this book to three related elements: a number, two letters (one upper one lower case) and a name. For example, p18 is Ar 'Ariadne', p6 is C 'Bing Crosby'.

The relationship between the numbers, letters and names is made clearer with the information that the book is based upon the Chemical Periodic Table; Ar is therefore Argon and C is Carbon. In a similar fashion to Patterson's other work, he has taken a 'ready-made' object, in this case a scientific chart, and invested it with a range of new meanings and associations. By introducing names of celebrities, mythological figures, artists and jargon, Patterson suggests new chemistries between the characters which are both personal and also deeply rooted in cultural canons and hierarchies.

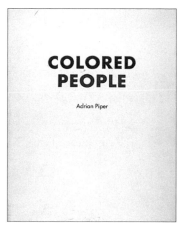
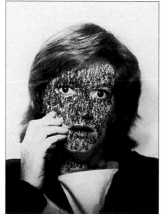

Coloured People by Adrian Piper, offset litho, black and white and colour, printed dust jacket, 292pp, soft cover.

This book represents a provocative examination about the degree to which perceptions of race and difference are embedded in our culture and language.

Sixteen self-selected men and women, from a range of racial groups, have collaborated with American artist Adrian Piper in this project by contributing eight photographs of themselves. Each photograph shows a posed facial description of a colloquial expression of mood. The eight sections of the book are organised according to these metaphors, such as, tickled pink, jaundiced yellow, black depression. In each case Piper has drawn onto the individual's face an ill-fitting area of the corresponding colour.

This treatment of the photograph has the effect of explicitly investigating the degree to which assumptions about colour and race structure our everyday language. Photographs such as the man standing in front of African masks, or the woman holding her camera in the act of taking a photograph suggest the penetration of these prejudices into the work of image-makers and our attitudes towards different cultures and history.

Two Oxford Reading Rooms by Joseph Kosuth, printed offset litho, soft cover, 108pp.

This book replicates the two installations which Joseph Kosuth devised for Book Works as part of The Reading Room project at the Taylor Institution and the Bodleian Library, Oxford University in 1994. It contains two texts 'The (Ethical) Space of Cabinets 7 & 8' located in the Voltaire Room of the Taylor Institution and 'Say: I do not know' in response to the Divinity School in the Bodleian Library. Kosuth's work over nearly 30 years has been a process of investigation into the relationship between art and philosophy and this book allows the reader to engage with these concerns in both its physical and textual form. As Kosuth invites the viewer actively to participate in his installations he requires that the reader play an active part in the way this book reveals its contents. The first decision is about which end of the book to start: it could be said that the book has no definitive beginning or end. Transparent pages with text are placed next to pages of photographs and can be turned to reveal the room in which this discussion originates, or pages which frame a passage can be turned to expose further commentaries, analyses or questions. By exploring the relationship between Voltaire's and John Locke's writings this complex book asks pertinent and serious questions about the location and use of knowledge and experience.

The Price of Words, Places to Remember 1-26 by Lily Markiewicz, printed offset litho, with a series of duotone images, 60pp, soft cover.

Combining a sequence of photographic images and twenty-six texts this book presents two parallel narratives. The photographs feature a series of moments passing as grains (possibly, sand) are poured into a metal bowl. These images of the grains pouring, filling, resting and piling into the bowl are interspersed between the reflective written statements. In these German-born artist Markiewicz asks personal questions about memory, history, territory, culture and language in relation to her own Jewish identity as part of the Post-Holocaust generation. This book is a philosophical and poetical consideration of these issues which offers hopes of 'becoming' and sensitively asks the reader to enquire into the difficult examination of the past.

Cecil Beaton – Stage and Film Designs
Charles Spencer

Based on Cecil Beaton's personal recollections, notebooks and sketchbooks, Charles Spencer's sympathetic and penetrating account investigates Beaton's contributions not only to the theatre but also to ballet, opera and film where his work has brought him great acclaim and recognition. The evolution and characteristic components of 'the Beaton style', with its celebration of English high society of the Edwardian era are recorded in a generous selection of illustrations which point to the deep and lasting impression his remarkable career has left on 20th-century stage design.

An Art & Design Monograph
305 x 252 mm, 128 pages
150 b/w ills, 20 colour
April 1995

David Mach

Scottish born artist David Mach rose to prominence in the early 80s with his remarkable large-scale sculpture projects, notably *Polaris*, the submarine made entirely from tyres exhibited at the South Bank Centre in London. His sculpture is characterised by his use of multiple components such as magazines, newspapers, matches, bottles, suggesting today's obsession with consumerism, and the resulting levels of manufactured surplus and waste. This monograph, published in collaboration with Newlyn Art Gallery in Cornwall presents a selection of his remarkable projects along with an indepth essay by Paul Bonaventura and interview with the artist conducted by Tim Marlow.

An Art & Design Monograph
305 x 252mm, 128 pages
Over 150 colour ills
July 1995

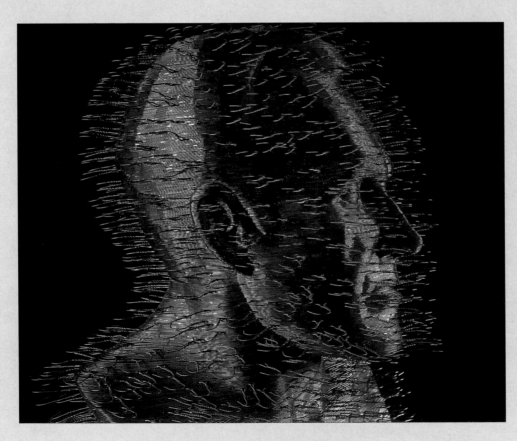

VALERY AND NATASHA CHERKASHIN

VISITING LONDON

Featured in Academy's recent *Post Soviet Art and Architecture*, Valery and Natasha Cherkashin, two of the leading performance/installation artists in Moscow, visited London at the end of November 1994. They held impromptu exhibitions in Kew Gardens, visited Antony Gormley at the Tate Gallery Turner Prize exhibition, 'bathed' their pictures in the fountain at Trafalgar Square, in the Thames and in the shower at the home of Gilbert & George.

Valery became director of the Museum Metropolitan, the conceptual museum of Moscow's underground transport system in the early 1990s, 'with its statues and reliefs, people and perspectives, red partisans and drug addicts, dirty marble and the most educated passengers in the world'. Along with Natasha, the main curator, he has arranged striking subterranean performances including the privitisation of statues from the revolutionary 30s in the Revolution Square station, 'weddings' between real people and bronze statues ('the love of the people for People's Art') and the arrangement of a beauty contest of statues adorned with sashes and crowns. These attempts to appropriate the official art of the revolutionary era for the post-modern age, personalise the impersonal and humourise the humourless, typify the work of many artists in this survey. The Cherkashins' visit to London followed a highly successful trip to the States where they organised an exhibition which attempted to recreate the atmosphere of Red Square in the Museum of Fine Arts, Santa Fe, New Mexico.

Post Soviet Art and Architecture, *edited by Alexey Yurasovsky and Sophie Ovenden, published by Academy Editions 1994, £17.95, 84 images mostly in colour. Contributors include Charles Jencks, Lisa Appignanesi, Elinor Shaffer, Alexander Rappaport, Andrey Tolstoy and Nadezhda Yurasovskaya.*

SUBSCRIPTIONS

| UK: | £10/4 issues |
| Europe: | £12/4 issues |

29 Poets Road
London N5 2SL

UNTITLED

A quarterly review of contemporary art

BRITISH ART
DEFINING THE 90S

Forced Entertainment, Marina and Lee *(photo Hugo Glendinning), see pp58-67*

Art & Design

BRITISH ART
DEFINING THE 90S

Keith Piper, Surveillances: Tagging the Other, *1992, still from computer animation (see pp48-57); OPPOSITE: John Keane*, New British Landscape, *1987, oil and mixed media on canvas, 243.8 x 182.9cm (see pp88-96)*

ACADEMY EDITIONS • LONDON

Acknowledgements

We would like to thank all the writers, artists and galleries who kindly lent us material and put so much energy into this issue of *Art & Design* on British Art.

Breaking Content from Form *pp6-19*: p6 Lisson Gallery, London; p8 Waddington Galleries, London; p9 the artist; p10 Victoria Miro, London; p12 Karsten Schubert, London; p13 Waddington Galleries; p14 Karsten Schubert (above), Anthony Reynolds (below); p16 Private Collection; p17 Antony Reynolds; p19 Lisson Gallery, London (above), Waddington Galleries (below); **Reclaiming the Subject, or Making a Case for the Angel** *pp20-27*: Essay published courtesy of the Pedro Oliveira Gallery, Porto, Portugal, images courtesy of the artist; p20 photo Pedro Oliveira; p25 photo Jay Jopling, London; **Matt's Gallery** *pp28-47*: Images courtesy of Matt's Gallery, London, this piece was prepared with the kind assistance of Robin Klassnik and Alison Raftery; **Eddie Chambers** *pp48-57*: Images courtesy of Eddie Chambers; **Performing Questions** *pp58-67*: Images courtesy of the performers; **Women's Voices** *pp68-75*: Images courtesy of the artists; **When are You Leaving?** *pp76-81*: p76 City Racing, London; p78 Interim Art, London (above), Stein Gladstone, New York (below); p79 the artist; p80 Centre for Contemporary Art, Glasgow (above and centre), the artist (below); **Parallel Structures** *pp82-87*: Courtesy of the artists: except pp84 and 86 Anthony Reynolds, London; **John Keane** *pp88-96*: Images courtesy of the artist and Angela Flowers Gallery, London, *p94*: Collection Trustees of the Imperial War Museum, London.

FRONT AND BACK COVER: Ian Davenport, Untitled (Poured lines, Blue)*, 1994, household paint on canvas, 213.4 x 213.4cm (Waddington Galleries, London)*
INSIDE COVERS: Antony Gormley, European Field*, 1993, terracotta, approximately 40,000 figures of variable size between 8 and 26 cm high, photo Jan Uvelius*

EDITOR: Nicola Kearton SUB-EDITOR: Stephen Watt
ART EDITOR: Andrea Bettella CHIEF DESIGNER: Mario Bettella DESIGNER: Toby Norman

First published in Great Britain in 1995 by *Art & Design* an imprint of
ACADEMY GROUP LTD, 42 LEINSTER GARDENS, LONDON W2 3AN
Member of the VCH Publishing Group
ISBN: 1 85490 229 6 (UK)

The Publishers and Editor do not hold themselves responsible for the opinions expressed by the writers of articles or letters in this magazine
Copyright of articles and illustrations may belong to individual writers or artists
Art & Design Profile 41 is published as part of *Art & Design* Vol 10 3/4 1995
Art & Design Magazine is published six times a year and is available by subscription

Distributed to the trade in the United States of America by
ST MARTIN'S PRESS, 175 FIFTH AVENUE, NEW YORK, NY 10010

Printed and bound in Italy

Contents

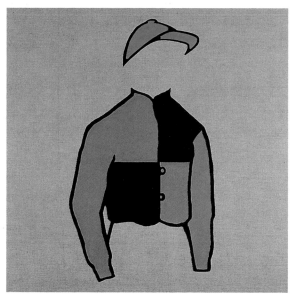

Mark Wallinger, Browns (Mr D.B. Brown), *1993, oil on linen, 110 x 110cm (see pp6-19)*

ART & DESIGN PROFILE No 41

BRITISH ART – DEFINING THE 90S

Art and Language, Portrait of VI Lenin with Cap, in the Style of Jackson Pollock III, *1980*

BREAKING CONTENT FROM FORM
ANDREW WILSON

Painting, like work executed in any medium in Britain today, can often seem to be most easily characterised by its bewildering diversity. Nevertheless, one direction in which painting has recently travelled reinterrogates the ways in which meaning can be created and communicated through the seemingly intractable and determining surfaces of Modernist painting. Work carried out in this vein, if of varied appearance and motivation, can be identified by a steadfast attention to the 'facts' of painting where at the same time a sense of content disengages, to a greater or lesser extent, from the subject. In these paintings the gaps which open up between subject and content – the 'how' and the 'what' – are bridged by the construction of meaning. One aspect of this development is the realisation that the pluralities of a Postmodernist culture do not constitute a reversal or death of Modernism (such as that which was heralded by the 'Trans-avanguardia' of the 80s), but that such a term describes more exactly a refabrication of Modernism, or, as Jean-François Lyotard has suggested, 'Modernity is constitutionally and ceaselessly pregnant with its Postmodernity'[1].

By extension, Michael Craig-Martin has stressed how the two fundamental attributes of art are to be found in the framing of a quality of thought and a quality of sight, reflecting the transformative act where an idea is presented as an object;

> 'the most essential characteristic of art, and the only really essential one . . . is an aspect of faith and an aspect of thought and, because it's a visual art, what it looks like, about the appearance of things. And those are the basic constituents of all visual art, all paintings . . . I don't use what I think of as a kind of obscuring technique. I try to do it by being as explicit as possible . . . I mean, art is clearly mysterious and I'm not at all interested in making something which is mystifying.'[2]

Such an outlook, as this statement reflects, draws attention to the necessity for a recognition of the difference between content and subject matter in the creation of a painting – where subject matter can be found in the facts of painting and an approach which is self-critical to those facts of painting, and the content located in that sense of mystery or thought that accompanies the act of making a painting.

What Craig-Martin describes is a painting which both takes account of a Greenbergian Modernist attachment to the elusive content of 'aesthetic value' and recognises those Minimalist prerogatives where the facts of painting become no more than what they are as part of real space, whilst recovering a division between subject matter and content. A Minimalist painting, such as Frank Stella's, while still exerting a self-critical attack on their means of expression, broke decisively with Greenbergian aesthetics by moving the painting into the world of real objects. Content became the paint which was its own subject matter, and by framing their own reality the division between subject matter and content was lost. Greenberg could not accept this move into real space as content, in his view, painting should not refer to anything outside the painting. Nevertheless, constituted by 'aesthetic value' – the experience of an emotion in front of the painting – content still existed as the result of a self-sufficient aesthetic system.

The move that Stella's painting embarked on at the end of the 50s – 'Frank Stella had found it necessary to paint stripes. There is nothing else in his painting . . . His stripes are the paths of brush on canvas. These paths lead only into painting'[3] – draws attention to this fact, where subject matter, as much as content, can only be found in the act of painting itself. That position, in which subject matter and content become indistinguishable, has now led to an anxiety over what to paint, and why; a point that was summed up when, faced by the paintings of Ian Davenport, the artist Liam Gillick proposed the suggestion that 'one of the most interesting things about this work is that Davenport bothers to do it at all.'[4] As a result, the necessity of such questioning has led to an increasing diversity of surfaces as content once again breaks free from the subject matter of paint and the act of painting.

If there is one factor that has determined the character of painting throughout the 20th century it can be recognised in the way that artists have negotiated a line between idea and the realisation of idea as image; the embodiment of creative transformation. At one extreme there is a concern for the reification of meaning within the invariably mute surfaces of a process that gives an appearance to painting that is resolutely non-figurative, and yet still has to figure content, still carry and project meaning. Alternatively, there is the desire to make images that are both about painting and about that paint's transference of subject and meaning to a figured subject which could also enact a discourse whose site is far from the palette and the surface of the painting.

What such a summing up proposes is that there is more than one Modernism. The relationship between subject and content in the work of Mondrian or Rodchenko is of a markedly different order to that found in paintings by Larry Poons or Morris Louis (or Frank Stella). In both cases the content is close to the subject matter of the painting, but the internal logic of the earlier

Michael Craig-Martin, Red Paintings, *1991, nine identical canvases, acrylic and gesso on canvas, 213.4 x 213.4 x 3.8cm, installation Waddington Galleries, London*

Alan Charlton, Four Walls Four Greys, *1991, installation the Louver Gallery, New York*

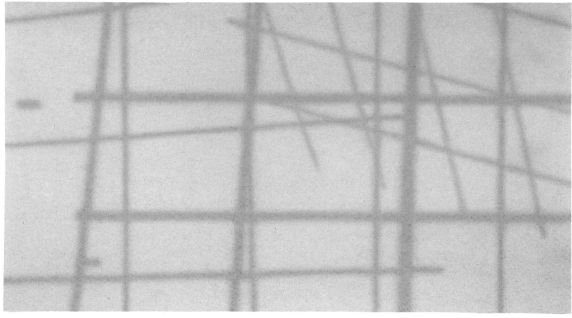

Brad Lochore, FROM ABOVE:
Untitled, *1993, oil on canvas, 140*
x 300cm; Shadow No 48, *1994,*
oil on canvas, 290 x 160cm

Modernism provides the means by which an externally directed message can be reified in its surface (and not just as a symbol of something), while the siting of Greenbergian Modernism's content in 'aesthetic value' disallows the possibility of such an external projection.

What is figured in the painting is an idea, and not the figuration of painting itself nor a figured image (or degrees of both). One aspect of which can be found in the painting of Alan Charlton who has been making grey paintings for over 25 years. Each painting is constructed, and could be said to be the result of an already determined internal logic, but although their subject matter resides in respect of this logic of construction their content makes contact with the mystery that occurs when an idea is transformed and realised as an object – as a made grey painting. Like Craig-Martin's recent paintings, Charlton's have always existed on that knife edge between clarity and mystery, but where no element of mystery is 'depicted' in the finished work. The 1975 'Fundamental Painting' exhibition in Amsterdam, which included Charlton as well as artists such as Gerhard Richter, Agnes Martin, Robert Ryman, Brice Marden and Robert Mangold, proposed a 'primary structure painting' whose attitude was characterised as one that was concerned 'with painting *qua* painting in a strict sense – on a flat plane, without representation and without image', the artists were portrayed as being 'involved first and foremost with the basic principle of painting', where 'the painting is what it is, it does not represent more than what is there to be seen.'[5]

Despite this appeal to fact, where content disappears into subject, Charlton does not exactly follow such a line. In one of his few published statements, he presented a quotation of Alberto Giacometti which at first glance perhaps sits uncomfortably with the overt reality of Charlton's grey paintings; 'The adventure, the great adventure, is to see something unknown appear each day, in the same face. That is greater than any journey around the world.'[6] What the choice of this statement underlines is that the making of a grey painting is not just about its making, but that there has to be a separation between that subject and the quality of making and seeing, just as there is a gap that has to be bridged when idea is presented as object;

> 'you see the painting and it is exactly what it is but when you stand in front of it, it is about somebody who has made a painting with a feeling. If you just stood in front of a painting and saw it completely in formal abstract ways I think you'd miss the point.'[7]

In the face of such thinking, the content of painting like Charlton's is bound up with the need to make meaning. Sited in the gap between idea and the realisation of idea as image, the questions that are asked of content, in this act of making meaning, become directed, not at the external form of something, but at an internal structuring of language. The retrospective of Malevich mounted at the Stedelijk Museum in Amsterdam a little over five years ago was significant in this respect. It deflected attention away from the resolutely non-figurative appearance of his Suprematist paintings and onto the defining character of the 'world without objects' captured within them – his non-objective Utopianism – in such a way that his late, 'figurative', paintings of 1928-34 could be reconsidered to be not an aberration, but as providing the key to the content of his earlier Suprematist paintings.

What this picture of Malevich underlines is the difference between the two 20th-century Modernisms – Greenberg's where content is found in aesthetic fulfilment of the subject matter and that of Malevich, and other avant-garde artists of the 20s and 30s, where content provokes a sort of anti-formalism in being too excessive for, and detached from the subject matter (and Greenberg attacked Malevich for this very reason). If anything, what distinguishes some of the best of painting in Britain (as elsewhere), at the moment, is a detachment of subject from content and the attempt to bridge that gap, as meaning is wrought, and the idea becomes paint. This prevailing attitude is not concerned with painting as such – with making paintings that are about paintings – but with finding the most adequate means for conveying a meaning, and this need not necessarily be through arranging paint on canvas. Some have come to painting from other activities, sculpture or the third area, such as Michael Craig-Martin or Gerard Hemsworth, others like Mark Wallinger or Keith Coventry still make paintings while following other pursuits; Wallinger has admitted to being both excited by the possibilities of painting and sceptical of its traditions.[8] None produce paintings because they just want to paint but because they want to communicate a meaning that is, in this instance, best delivered by painting. Similarly, just as a non-figurative painting can be read in representational terms, so too can the representational become non-figurative. Seen in this way – faced by the twin demands of subject and content – such terms become little more than barely meaningful labels.

Such a disjunction between subject and content provides the means of locating those artists where slippages occur between the material appearances of their paintings and the content that is locked within their surface. Paintings by Brad Lochore, Glenn Brown or Simon Linke, each in their own ways, stand as the result of a negotiation which is carried out as much between subject and content, as it is between painting and its place in the contemporary world. In questioning the implication that photography provides an impartial objective recording of reality, these paintings go far beyond the usual perception of the problem of painting recovering a role in the face of photography's power, and the supposed ease by which 'aesthetic value' can be displaced by mechanical replication. Each of these three artists offer an image of something that we recognise, and are familiar with, and yet each takes the ground from under our feet by having moved content away from the ostensible subject matter. Lochore presents us with paintings of shadows (but they are not), Brown with paintings of photographs of paintings (but they are not) and Linke with paintings of magazine advertisements

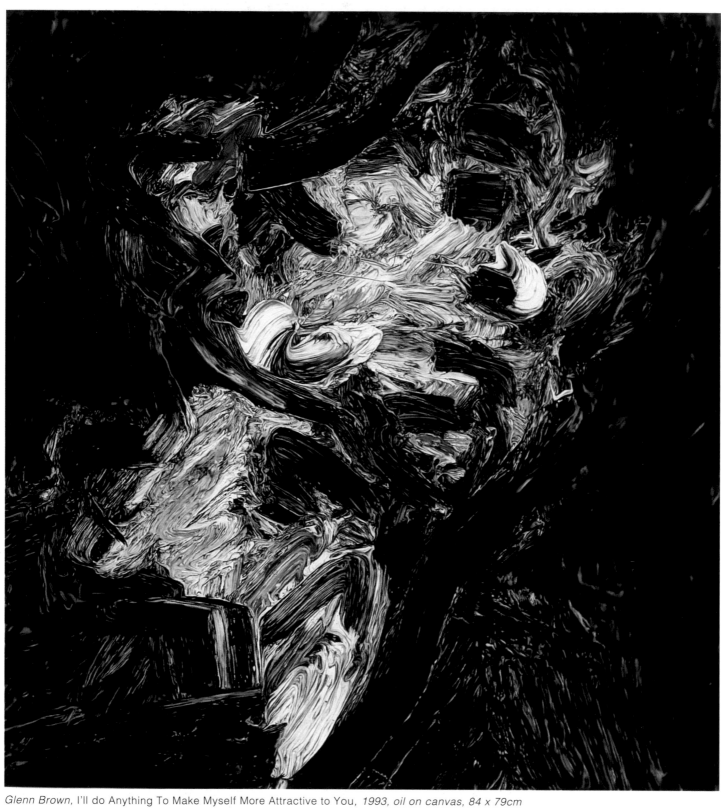

Glenn Brown, I'll do Anything To Make Myself More Attractive to You, *1993, oil on canvas, 84 x 79cm*

Fiona Rae, Untitled (green, blue, orange), *1994, oil on canvas, 198.3 x 193.5cm*

FROM ABOVE: Keith Coventry,
White Abstract (Cucumber
Sandwich), *1994, oil on canvas,
gessoed wood and canvas, 38.7
x 47 x 5cm; Gerard Hemsworth,*
Kiss my arse, *1994, acrylic on
canvas, 213 x 244cm*

(but they are not). Each does not set out to make a painting but to negotiate content through painting.

In his painting Lochore figures various configurations of shadows as an imprint or trace of something that is out of sight, or has moved on. Insubstantial, where the painting is substantial, the shadow becomes the object's double. However, what Lochore actually presents is a created fiction, which is built on the shifting sands of perception, where the painted shadows do not provide the narrative record of actual shadows but of images arrived at from the projection of a slide (the light by which shadows are cast) which has itself been computer-generated. Lochore, in offering such a feint to the beholder, steers a line between the reality of the painting and the fiction of its content. This demands the action of sight to attempt to place something which is always going to be out of view of the beholder, whose recognition of what is seen is constantly undermined. As a result, the shadows in the paintings oppose their content which attempts, perceptually, to pin them down and find the object of which they are a surrogate.

In a similar way Glenn Brown purloins a photographic image of a painting, from a book or poster, and proceeds to paint a copy of that photographic image. Impasto and tonal qualities are flattened and made opaque, approximating the surface sheen of the photographic emulsion. In contrast to this, Simon Linke's paintings of advertisements from the pages of Artforum appear to revel in proclaiming themselves as paintings, rather than printed sheets of paper, 'stranded midway,' as Stuart Morgan presciently observed, 'between objects and idea,'[9] between subject and content. The shock of seeing Linke's paintings for the first time is rather akin to seeing Mondrian's paintings – with all their painterly imperfections and hesitations – after only seeing them in cheap reproduction where the nuance of the paint is flattened out and the empirical, intuitively wrought compositions become purely programmatic, or mechanically designed. In negotiating a space between their source material and its presentation as a painting, both Brown and Linke are questioning the closeness of content to the physical facts of the painting. Linke's paintings certainly provide a commentary to what is figured within them – the art world of the 80s read through the reflecting glass of their advertisements – but much more than this, those gestural surfaces upset the typographic clarity of the printed advertisement.

As a result of approximating the uninflected look of a photograph, whose subject is a gestural, impastoed, painting, Brown effects a denial of his paintings as painting (it is of a photographic image of a painting) and as photograph (look, it is a painting) – the 'aesthetic value' locked in the gestural nature of the original paintings is annulled, even though Brown's painting are as finely wrought as a Northern Renaissance miniaturist. His recreations of Dali paintings emphasise this sense of paranoia where the sleek surfaces of the original are already close to that of the photographic reproduction. Content here is about reality and how it can be perceived and presented, not as the reality of painting and its processes but how those fictions upset a careful ordering of reality.

What Brown and Linke, in common with most of these artists, recognise is the determining artificiality of painting. Any image that results is something which has been wholly fabricated and is perhaps even something of a contrivance. To this extent meaningful content can only survive if it cuts itself away from the subject matter of the painted surface, to seek refuge as a mental construct, which may indeed have determined the appearance of that surface but which also allows for another life.

In 1989, Fiona Rae described her work as 'kind of phoney abstract.'[10] Described in this way her paintings could be said to inhabit a limbo of ambiguity, making no claims for what they stand for within any value structure of abstract painting, or indeed, for how they appear in any formal or colouristic sense. But then they are not abstract paintings in that Greenbergian sense. They luxuriate in an anti-formalism, in a clash of technique and effect, where a disordering of pictorial unity or compositional sense can achieve coherence. Her repertoire of artistic devices, both invented and translated from other artists, unpicks the language of formalism by feeding it with the complexities of the contemporary experiences of signs clashing and competing for attention. They are not figurative (although elements within them can be more or less recognised) and they are not abstract. Instead they are phoney in that they play with the language of abstraction whilst also acting out a picture of it. By casting off abstraction, by means of quotation, she is then able to disengage herself from the image and from the demands of surface and technique. Given such a play of moves, the content becomes part of the process of making meaning out of disorder, fuelled by the traditions of Modernism.

The door paintings of Gary Hume, whether painted uniformly in an institutional magnolia or hung together in a diverse combination of sizes, design and colour, had, as he admitted, 'no essential core of meaning . . . they remain an empty sign.'[11] Painted as if 'doors', these paintings happened to be formed in terms of a language that challenged any possibility of a reification of meaning. Content seemed irredeemably lost in their unforgiving blank surfaces, so that they were neither 'abstract' nor 'doors'. By 1992, Hume had began to attack their silken surfaces, complicating, defacing and dirtying them. The paintings that followed have presented recognisable images in a slick but degraded way – Patsy Kensit, with her thumb in her mouth, or Jesus – and use the same expanses of gloss paint as the doors. Although adopting a disguise of clarity, these paintings stand as an anamorphic projection of those earlier door paintings (just as in one painting Tony Blackburn's head can be seen emerging from a shamrock). The self-critical nature of Modernism determines that each mark, each brush stroke, stands as itself, as a representation of itself (and as a record of that means of a representation). By not representing something that lies outside

Gary Hume, Dolphin Painting IV, *1991, gloss paint on MDF board, four panels overall 222 x 643cm*

Mark Wallinger, Race, Class, Sex, 1992, oil on canvas, four paintings each 230 x 300cm (photo Gareth Winters)

the painting in the real world (whilst making the painting real in itself), the brush stroke can't fail in being an empty signifier. Although the door paintings showed the possibility of upsetting such a state by proposing a painting which is a painting of a door, which is actually just a painting, Gary Hume's recent achievement has consisted in definitively opening a fissure that allows such a state of painting to continue, whilst also presenting a content that exists beyond the painting's own sense of subject.

Ian Jeffrey, writing about Lisa Milroy's paintings of objects arranged in rows and grids, suggested that something similar was occurring; that the content was neither in the facts of the painting nor in the image portrayed. What 'is experienced is not the thing in isolation, but the relationship between that and this painted image and beyond that to "things" and words. What is "real" in these pictures happens in the interstices, in the spaces in between, and in the act or idea of connecting.'[12] Recently, too, Milroy's painting has undergone a shift, and is now concerned with paintings of landscapes, crowds, urban snapshots of Tokyo and Japanese wrapping paper. Not only is the ordering preordained, but the images also have an internal narrative history that is already present because the white ground of the earlier paintings has been exchanged. The act of 'picturing' something has been replaced by the creation of spatial illusion which attacks the Modernist premise on which her earlier paintings were based. Or seems to. Is not a 'picturing' still taking place that, like Hume's *Tony Blackburn*, does not attempt at a capturing of verisimilitude but, by being conceived in terms of a language of visual signs, is instead still attempting to find a 'reality' in the spaces in between objects as between the image and paint?

For Craig-Martin, the beholder's viewing becomes itself the act of transforming an object (the painting) into meaning. The painting's content exists in this act of transformation, which is also one of interpretation and perception. The painting, as an object, can then demystify the 'mystery' of perception which is a content external to itself and yet reliant on its subject. His recent paintings issue from a sculptural perspective, bringing to the foreground the perceptual materiality of the painting, addressing the role of reality, illusion and truth as it might be revealed in the particular physical presences that his paintings hold: 'I have wanted to bring the experience of a work so close to the surface, one can watch it happening. That is the subject of my work.'[13]

Like Michael Craig-Martin, Gerard Hemsworth was also originally a sculptor who has turned to painting as a way of furthering conceptual concerns of perception. As Nicholas de Ville has explained, Hemsworth's move towards painting, and away from his sculptural and photo-text work, was carried through as a response to finding a way to 'reassert the visual as the source of imagined meaning within the framework of sceptical distancing that is inherent in conceptual art. This forced the . . . dispersal of the subject and the return to representation.'[14] His recent paintings make this split more acute. The image shows a framing that is voided, both of subject and (like Hume's doors) of content

which pushes the spectator away from contact with either, even though the image is something that can be easily recognised because the borders of Hemsworth's void are themselves depthlessly empty. And yet the voided spaces have to be 'filled' in such a way that the beholder 'can watch it happening'.

Such a perspective recognises that painting is, all at once, an idea, an object and the result of the transformation of one realised in the form of the other, as a sense of becoming which is also grounded on an issue of making meaning. Mark Wallinger's paintings of jockey colours, the adoption of a horse as *A Real Work of Art*, or his various paintings of thoroughbred horses might suggest an activity that is remote from arguments surrounding Modernism. However his work – whether it is painting or not – has always been concerned with registering this split, in the act of representation, between subject and content between reality, artifice and 'aesthetic value':

'By choosing a racehorse, I am presenting something for contemplation which functions as a history of aesthetics in microcosm . . . Along with the idea of the artist denoting something as an artwork, there has always been in my work an investigation into the nature of representation, a disjunction between what a work appears to want to say and what is said. Are we talking about reality here or are we talking about artifice?'[15]

Because of this disjunction, when we approach paintings, such as those by Wallinger of jockey colours belonging to people named Brown, the experience doesn't cease being a retinal one but, in addition, belongs within the conceptual realm as well. The painting is understood as idea, object and in terms of the transformational passage between the two. Like Duchamp's malic moulds, these hats and jackets are waiting for the illuminating gas, not only of the unfigured person within the painting, but also that of the beholder so that their content and meaning can be unlocked. In contrast to this Greenberg's Modernism relied on the isolation of content and subject issuing from a painting's purely optical dimension.

In this respect, the phrase 'conceptual realism' was coined, by Greg Hilty in 1988, as a means of describing the work of Tony Benn and Clair Joy, among others, in which 'the language of painterly realism' is allied to an attempt 'to give solid, sensuous form to conceptual concerns.'[16] This cuts both ways, and one of my aims has been to show how abstraction, freed from, the constraints of Greenbergian formalism on one side and, on the other, the demands of a Minimalist tradition, can in effect be employed to conceptual ends; that in the act of creative transformation, where idea becomes object, it is possible for the content not only to split away from but also cannibalise the concerns of painting's subject matter.

Keith Coventry's paintings, in their misuse of formalist convention, embrace such a view. Meaning, in his representations of housing estate plans as Suprematist paintings or in his monochrome portraits of the Royal family, does not exist within the

Modernist essentialist discourse on the creative act, the formalist reading of composition or the perennial idea of the death of painting (however much they might look like it). Instead, through his twisting of content, and analytical presentation of Modernism's historicist forms, meaning is held and communicated by a mute visual sign. The ability for meaning to attach itself to something as barren as a monochrome surface can then be held up as a witness against the historicism and essentialism that had previously defined the course and character of Modernism, where meaning had been effectively exchanged for prosaic, self-contained, wholly self-referential discourse.

Andrew Wilson is an art historian and critic whose writing has appeared in many magazines and exhibition catalogues. He was London correspondent for Forum International, *1991-93, and is currently completing a PhD at the Courtauld Institute on Patrick Heron.*

Notes

1 Jean-François Lyotard, 'Rewriting Modernity', *The Inhuman,* Polity Press, Cambridge, 1993, p 25.

2 Michael Craig-Martin, from an unpublished interview with Rod Stoneman (1986); see Lynne Cooke, 'The Prevarication of Meaning', *Michael Craig-Martin a Retrospective, 1968-1989*, Whitechapel Art Gallery, London, 1989, pp 11 and 12.

3 Carl Andre, 'Preface to Stripe Painting', *Sixteen Americans,* Dorothy Miller ed, Museum of Modern Art, New York, 1959, p 76.

4 Liam Gillick, 'Ian Davenport', *Artscribe International,* issue 80, March-April, 1990, p 57.

5 *Fundamentale Schilderkunst/Fundamental Painting,* Stedelijk Museum, Amsterdam, 1975, pp 11-13.

6 Ibid, artist's statement.

7 Andrew Wilson, 'For me it has to be done good', Alan Charlton interviewed, London, June 25 1991, *Art Monthly,* September, 1991, p 17.

8 See Mark Wallinger interviewed by Paul Bonaventura, 'Turf Accounting', *Art Monthly,* April, 1994, p 4.

9 Stuart Morgan, 'Simon Linke, Twilight Zone', *Artscribe International,* issue 64, Summer, 1987, p 53.

10 Fiona Rae, from a conversation, September 1989, *The British Art Show,* The South Bank Centre, London, 1990, p 92.

11 Gary Hume, ibid, p 66.

12 Ian Jeffrey, *Lisa Milroy,* Nicola Jacobs Gallery, London, 1988.

13 Michael Craig-Martin, 'April 1991' *Michael Craig-Martin,* Musée des Beaux-Arts, Andre Malraux, Le Havre, 1991, p 12.

14 Nicholas de Ville, *Gerard Hemsworth: Self-Portraits 1977-1987,* Matt's Gallery, London, 1988.

15 Mark Wallinger interviewed by Paul Bonaventura, op cit, p 7.

16 Greg Hilty, 'Your Kiss is Sweet', *Land,* Riverside Studios, London, 1988.

FROM LEFT: Simon Linke, Untitled, *1993, oil on canvas, 182.8 x 182.8cm (photo Stephen White); Lisa Milroy,* Flowers, *1993, oil on canvas, 101.6 x 101.6cm*

Antony Gormley, (foreground) Lock, *1994, lead, fibreglass, plaster, air, 92 x 59 x 127cm, (background)* Passage, *1993, concrete, 36 x 44 x 229cm, installation view Pedro Oliveira Gallery, Porto, Portugal, 1994 (photo Antonio Pinto)*

ANTONY GORMLEY: RECLAIMING THE SUBJECT OR MAKING A CASE FOR THE ANGEL

ANDREW RENTON

'The angel, however, resembles all from which I have had to part: persons and above all things. In the things I no longer have, he resides. He makes them transparent, and behind all of them there appears to me the one for whom they are intended.' Walter Benjamin

It will always have begun with an absence or a space. A hollowed or left space, where something has been removed. The absence of the thing itself marked as a thing itself. The absented subject marks itself as a subject precisely because it is absent. It is a sign of itself. Such is the sculpture of Antony Gormley: with constant reference to a body, there is no body. And yet more than a point of reference, even the non-figurative sculpture of Antony Gormley is figured by the body. It is marked by the way a body might approach such an object. That is to say, if sculpture is to be understood, inevitably, by the way it invites a relationship to the viewing body, Gormley's sculpture insists on a form of presence-in-absence, where the viewer assumes the place of the sculptor and his body. The viewer is embodied in the process, filling the particularised space (the 'air' so specified in Gormley's work) of the object of contemplation.

More (or less) than a constructed space, it is an evacuated space, which allows a mental projection into the work on the part of the viewer. The projection is made available by a formal sense of material space. The term itself is all but tautological, but insists on the made space – an enforced space, perhaps – being rendered in the presence of the viewer.

The sculpture, then, appears to embrace a form of figuration. But this is not an illusion of resemblance, rather it is one of deferred reference; it is not like the body, it is from the body. Whatever illusion is conveyed by Gormley's sculpture, it is clearly derived from a specific body, where that body has been removed. In other words, the sculpture is made from the inside outwards, as opposed to the conventions of outside in.

In order to uncover this renewed embodiment, the body must be covered over. The object only emerges in stages, as the body is cast and removed. What remains is not the similitude of the death mask, seeking a moment of uncanny resemblance, but a secondary stage of overworking. The covering over of the body is a protection, encasement and mediation. It comes to define the limits of what was once inside.

However, just as the lead is contoured to the shape of the body that was once there, so that body moves outside of itself, as it were, to make itself up again. Resemblance, here, is cursory.

Such a method of manufacture, with its use of malleable material, gives way to a deferred imaging – a defacing, perhaps, where the body comes to represent bodies other than itself. What is actually revealed on the surface of the sculpture, with its sealed sections, is something that never attempts to represent the body, and could only exist as a sign of its (former) enclosure.

The obligation of the artist is not to re-create himself, but to generate enough distance between himself and his own object. That distancing process might be seen as the addressing of the subject, where the artist must position himself in relation to his own object seen as a trace commentary of his present self, and returning such an interpretation, in the form of praxis, back upon the object.

The object, then, is the site of the subject, rather than the subject itself. It becomes the object of contemplation by providing formal stasis within the fluctuating of vision and perception.

The specificity of the body is always then abstracted. It is *every* body. And it is not. Significantly, in the past few months, Gormley has developed something of a departure in his work by making a couple of pieces, one of which is called *Lost Subject*, which are specifically of himself. The universalised mode in which he has comfortably worked for so many years has been punctuated by the unique declarations of making – a kind of realised bearing witness, where the lead is beaten directly over a body cast. It is as though the encasement is enforcing a more profound engagement with its originating body. It does not wish to leave the body.

All but an abnegation of embodiment, by refusing to swerve away from uncanny resemblance, such an object must serve as an incomplete, heroic monument to the rest of Gormley's work. Incomplete, because it chooses not to differ or defer. It chooses not to stray too far from the body, hardly troping at all. This is a resisted embodiment, for all its specificity.

In this way, the more specific the sculpture becomes, the more it resembles its maker, the more it becomes an enabler, a demystifier for the subject of his work. The absolute figuration allows for abstraction in the other works. Objective specificity will come to confirm the universalisation of the body.

The primary trope here is not metaphor, however, but metonymy. We are not concerned here with what the thing looks like (the point of departure) or what the thing stands as, or for (the point of comparison). Rather, in Gormley's work there is a qualitative substitution always at work. There is an idea of embodiment; a proposed embodiment, which is offered in lieu of

Antony Gormley, A Case for an Angel II, *1990, plaster, fibreglass, lead, steel, air, 197 x 858 x46cm*

a constantly deferred promise of unity. Embodiment is always a point of reference and proposed construction, rather than a celebration of mass. For Gormley, mass and visual weight are different measures indeed.

Ineluctably physical, Gormley's figures nevertheless deny a certain degree of mass, of physical presence, by suggesting their role as substitutes for the real thing. The very title – *Case for an Angel* – offers a clue to the kind of substitution that is taking place here. In Judaic tradition, the angel is rarely embodied, but exists in a singular state, with an obligation to achieve a single aim. The angel is a messenger, and having delivered his message fades away. In kabbalistic and midrashic tradition, angels are represented as being created moment by moment to sing a single praise to God – a momentary spark. To define the angel, to speak in the theological, one must speak in the negative. The presence, the angel, is defined in terms of what it is not.

According to these terms, the angel may be seen as a carrier, or disseminating device, rather than an object of contemplation in itself. Since the Renaissance at least, the representation of the angel has never questioned the possibility of translating the unseeable into readily recognisable forms. But as the textual dialogue between Walter Benjamin and Gershom Scholem reveals, the image of the angel is always about to fade away.

In this way, the only way to represent the angel is by point of reference. For Gormley, too, there is no revelation or enunciation, but a bearing witness to the calm after such an appearance. And by the time we come to the figure, it has always already delivered its message.

Similarly, if the *Case for an Angel* marks the absence of the figure, encasing the place where the angel once was, may also be seen in prophetic terms, as a kind of projected, anticipatory trace; that is, where the angel may yet come to rest.

This projected trace is prevalent in Gormley's work, as it is one of the ways that an object is presented in a form of incompleteness. This metonymic suggestion of the whole cannot, by definition, accommodate the whole. If Gormley's sculpture is presented as the trace of something, it must also be seen, at the same time, as the possibility of something to come. This is achieved by the maker retaining the visibility of 'work' – the work at work – whilst he is seen to withdraw from the work.

Such a withdrawal is both physical and metaphysical. The physical is a manifestation of the artist's body as it extricates itself from the act of making within, to the act making without. The secondary process of the metaphysical occurs in this movement outwards. By moving outside of himself, as it were, the artist sets some distance between the making of the work and the effect that the work might generate.

This withdrawal is, of course, a form of completion, but occurs prior to completion. It is a completion where parameters of shape, weight and mass are defined to allow an indeterminate element to occur within the work. Completion, then, comes in the form of projection and introspection on the part of the viewer. There is a material and temporal gap which has been left where perception will take place.

The gap or marked space for perception is posited in another way in Gormley's *Field* pieces. Up to 40,000 clay figures, shaped in the hand by groups (families) of people, stare blankly, openly up at the viewer. It is an imponderable sight, simply due to the extent of the labour involved in the accumulation. *Field* demarcates time as well as space. Even within the restricted visual access offered by the artist (the work is only visible through the threshold of a theatrical 'fourth wall'), the eye cannot assimilate the extent of all that individuation. The uniqueness of each piece is countered by the number of pieces presented. The eye wavers between the field and its constituents. *Field* looks like it took time to make: it takes time to see what it looks like.

The sculpture is reinvested with the subject of making and consequential belonging. More than the communal assemblage of parts, the process Gormley establishes with his co-workers is one of regenerated subjectivity, rather than submission to a single idea. There is a whole, but it is hard to come upon. For the maker(s) it is hard to imagine; for the viewer it is hard to see.

There will always be a difference between what the work appears to be and its internal(ised) essence. The visual negotiation of Antony Gormley's work, for the viewer, is a reflection of the action of the artist – a delayed re-action or re-enactment. The working of the work, the way the work literally works out of itself is resistant to visualisation. This working out, or perhaps, working outwards, indicates a direction for the work, its emanation.

Resistance might be seen as a way of constructing an object in a synecdochial state, where completion is never offered for ethical reasons. The body cannot be completed because it cannot be contemplated in all its multivalency. In this way, the consistent reference to the body, the renewed figure in Gormley's work, is not a sign of visual impoverishment, but one of motion and flux.

And yet Gormley offers stilled bodies; bodies where movement is seen to be slowed. They become seeable in this decrescendo. Movement is suggested as if in the blink of an eye. It might be argued, then, that there must always be at least two figures in the frame as a relational act, but this is beside the point. Even the single body suggests others and other potentialities for movement. Between one pause and another, one stilled body creates another. All the while begging the question, If the body is so stilled, then how did it come to rest here?

Not only stilled, but enclosed, the body is never represented, despite impressions. Indeed, what is before the viewer is in the realm of impressions – the body pressed into lead, into concrete. Each material yields to the body, inevitably, in different ways. But it is always the material at the service of embodiment, never an immediate, descriptive act of likeness. Material is not transformed, turned or hidden.

Comparing disparate pieces such as *Close*, a prostrate, face-

Antony Gormley, Close II, 1993, lead, fibreglass, plaster, air, 27 x 201x174cm

Antony Gormley, Lost Subject I, 1994, lead, fibreglass, air, 25 x 145 x 228cm

Antony Gormley, FROM ABOVE: Seeds IV, 1993, lead, unit size 3.5 x 1.1cm; Passage, 1993, concrete, 36 x 44 x 229cm; Baring Light III, 1990, plaster, fibreglass, lead, rubber, air, 16 x 41 x 27cm

down lead body-case and *Passage*, a concrete block, draws distinct implications of the body. The former offers a more direct reference, not only to a body but a situation. It refers as much to where an event might have taken place as to a body which acts or is acted upon. The latter generates a potentially cool Modernist object which either encloses or distances itself from the body. The paradox, of course, is that this, too, is a synecdochial encasement, where negative impressions constitute the whole.

This distancing is doubly complex, because of the demands the sculpture makes of the viewer. Where does, say for example, she (a particular other, antithetical to the embodiment we see before us) stand? A positioning would appear to be crucial – not simply of the object but of the viewer in relation to it. There are claims for the materiality of sculpture which demand distance and the contemplation of mass. On the other hand, Gormley demands an intimacy of his viewer, because of the reflected intimacy of his own body's relation to the object, as well as the demands of scale, where the viewer must read the interruptions in the surface, rather than what is offered as a whole.

Again, where is she, this viewer? Where could one who is only defined negatively in relation to what is before her possibly position herself? The difficulty lies at the moment, or still point, of recognition in what remains of the body before her. Because that body will be so categorically other, 'she' will have to find other points of connection. And yet the body will always be other. It is mute, but were it to speak more than the vibrations of a pulse, it would define itself in terms of being seen by the viewer.

She says, 'There but for the grace of . . . , I might have been.' The conditions of evasion, the terms in which the viewer defines where she differs from the object of contemplation, are to be perceived in these interruptions, blanks or lacunae. There is no way to read the surface. She interprets the work just as she is about to turn away from it.

Perhaps, then, there is another reversal of a Modernist trend here. Whereas the exclusion of the subject in favour of the fact of the object in Modernist terms is crucial, Gormley is positing a Late-Modernist position where that exclusion has been so successful as to be almost semantically self-defeating. If the artwork has been compressed into a manifestation of itself, there will be closure to the revelation of experience. The demands made by the aura of the work of art would then be limited to an internalised rhetoric of abstraction.

In the absence of experience something must always fill the vacuum. The lesson of Modernism might be that what fills the vacuum is, of necessity, a self-generating, self-referential loop feeding the construction and reconstruction of the object.

One may posit Gormley's working method as a counterpoint to the anxious realisation of subjectless creation. The accumulation of lead bullet shapes which becomes *Seeds* is a manifestation of that anxiety turned upon itself as a fruitful site of regeneration.

These stages of accumulation (manufacture) and presence (arrangement) coexist in an obligation beyond mass.

Gormley's objects – even these tiny things – are literally bodies of evidence, where the internalisation is rendered visible, where the subject of making is redeemed.

This reversal not only opens the work to a narrative beyond itself, but retains a position in terms of the performative aspect of a work of art. The subject of the work – the renewed subject – is the amalgamation of the history of making with a history of being. It is clear that the object will tell its own tale of coming into being, of being made. But whose history of being? Of having already been made?

To suggest that Antony Gormley's sculptures refer either to a specific or to a generalised body is to deny their ability to refer to both. Their subject is a body and the body; a place and this place. The movement from the point of origin to the point of arrival (the initial siting and subsequent sighting of the work) is a twin movement from the general to the specific, from the specific to the universal. On the one hand, the new object could not be from anything but the body of the sculptor, whilst on the other hand, he has effaced himself. He has literally taken away his face.

And yet, Antony Gormley's body is not a sculptural template, but a living sight of action and being. It is not, then, a question of scale, but a more problematic definition of presence, or 'facing' – making a face and facing up. Surfacing is, of course, the superficial activity of the sculpture. Putting a face to something is an attempt to isolate and stabilise the internalised subject of the work. The viewer seeks definition from within abstraction, the sculptor seeks an equivalent point of closure. What the artist seeks, is the determination of a moment against which this, and countless other moments, might be set. The sculpture is, then, a pause in the artist's expression.

The subject of the object, as it were, then comes to rest outside the object itself. Yet, it does not fall too far from the body or embodiment. The subject constantly refers to the body, in the sense that it refers to it with repeated takes or perspectives. The subject of the work of art becomes the reappraisal of the body; not simply in a manifestation of physical potentialities and contortions, but in terms of points of reception. There are moments and places where the body can only be defined in terms of the body it is not.

What the sculpture of Antony Gormley appears to achieve is a refuting of the notion of a lost subject. Certainly the subject is hard to come upon, but it appears to have fallen just beyond the body in seeking another. The body becomes again what it once was, a messenger with singular purpose, making itself anew from one moment to the next.

Andrew Renton is a writer and curator living in London.

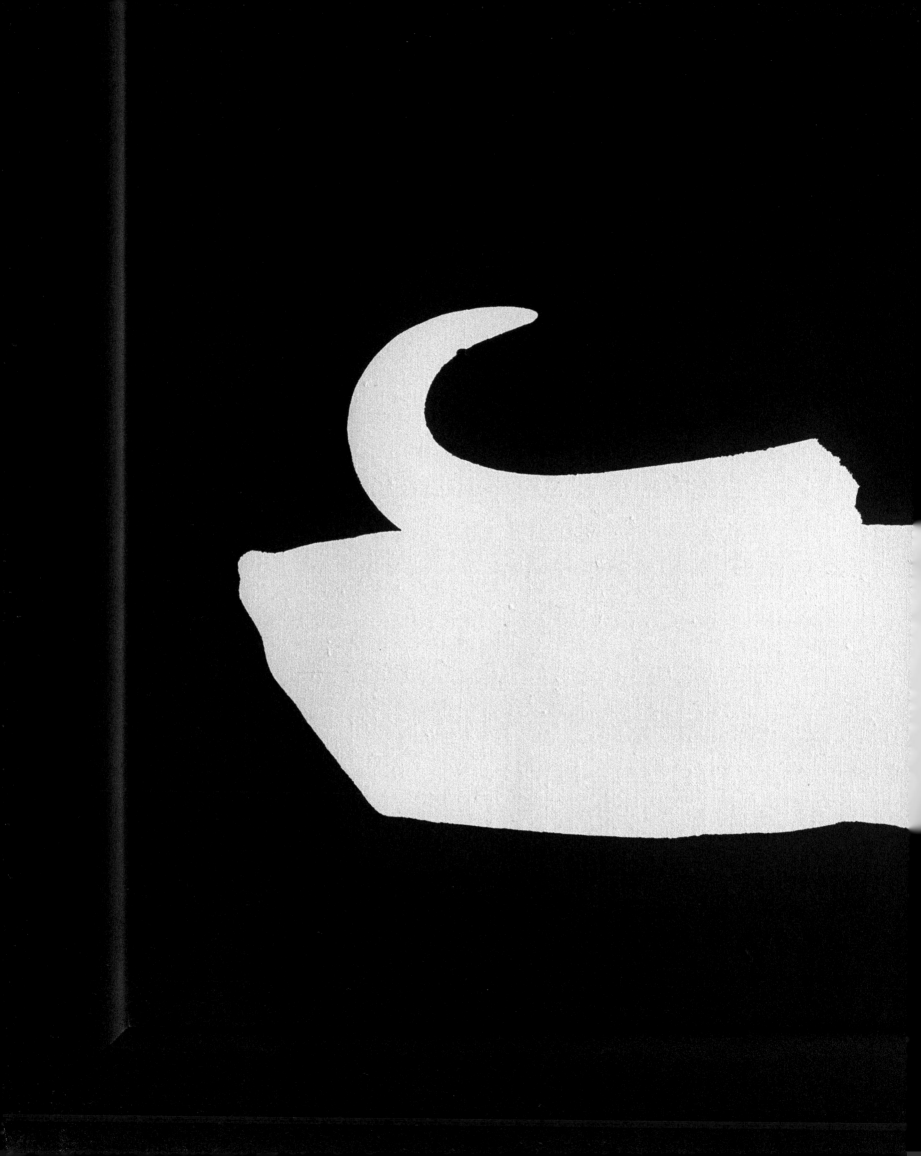

MATT'S GALLERY
JEFFREY KASTNER

Evolutionary changes are always easier to identify when they're completed rather than when they're occurring. The DIY culture in which today's young British artists operate seems so established, so fully formed, that it's tempting to see their broad strategic programme – peer group collaboration, utilising alternative venues away from the traditional centres of art world power, purposeful ambivalence about the gallery and dealer 'establishment' – as largely distinct from that which preceded it.

There's no question that the contemporary art scene of the mid-90s is a product of the art market crash and burn of the late-80s and the attendant decrease in institutional support available to the generation of artists just then beginning to emerge from the warmth and security of the art school cocoon. Yet, there are earlier precedents within the sweep of recent British art history for the kind of self-reliance and individual initiative which characterises today's environment for contemporary art in Britain. One of the most visible and longest lasting of these is Matt's Gallery, which has, under the guidance of its founder and director, Robin Klassnik, produced shows in a uniquely artist-friendly environment for 15 years.

Tucked away behind a heavy door in a row of unremarkable warehouse buildings in London's East End, the Matt's Gallery of today is a large complex incorporating an exhibition area, reception, office and storage. While this space in Copperfield Road is only a mile or two distant from Klassnik's original space in his studio at Martello Street, where Matt's Gallery was located from its inception in 1979 until 1991, it's worlds away from the original in scale and temperament. Klassnik's temperament, however, remains much the same as it was when, as a young practising artist dissatisfied with the exhibition opportunities in London, he decided to short-circuit the traditional gallery system and strike out on his own.

'I started in September of 1979,' Klassnik recalls. 'It took me two or three years to get going – I had been toying with the idea of starting a gallery but didn't really have the guts to do it.' An artist who had been showing regularly in Britain, Klassnik had also found an audience in Eastern Europe. 'In Poland, I came into contact with "unofficial" galleries – what we would have called "alternative" galleries if we had had any. I had shown here at the ICA and Whitechapel, but I also had a feeling that something was very wrong. I didn't like the way one was treated, although my expectations of an exhibition were probably very, very small compared with what people expect now from galleries.'

It was in Poland that Klassnik met Jaroslaw Kozlowski, an artist and teacher who had recently opened a gallery called Akumulatory 2 in Poznan. On the strength of one of Klassnik's mail art pieces to which Kozlowski had contributed, the Polish gallery director invited him to mount an exhibition in 1975. 'Kozlowski had this space within the students' union building which he used once a month for three or four days,' Klassnik remembers. 'He'd invite an artist to show a piece of work for two or three hours a day, for three days and then take it down – end of story.

'When I went to Poland I didn't know what to expect,' he continues. 'I knew (my show) was opening at five pm and I'd done it all and I was just sat there and I thought I'd just wait for the people. Then the director came in and said, "Are you ready?" And I said, "Ready for what?" He wanted to know if everything was OK, if I was happy. That really touched me. He was actually not going to let anyone in until I was satisfied. And then the people finally came in, and we looked at the work and talked about it. That was a completely new experience for me.'

At this point, in the mid-70s, there were very few comparable venues for artists in London, says Klassnik. 'None really. There was Air Gallery and ACME had a gallery, but I think that ceased in 1981. The scene was of one desperately trying to get a show at the Serpentine in their Summer Shows; that or the Whitechapel Open. I had spent a year organising open studios for Space with Alexis Hunter – we had 18 studio blocks and buses and everything, just like they do open studios now, but I became quite dissatisfied with it because there was no quality and I am interested in quality. It was the same in some ways with the work I was making. I was doing a lot of mail art, pieces which incorporated things sent to me, actually 'done' by the community. A lot of the work was participatory, it required the general public, but I was becoming disillusioned with that as well, probably because of this quality issue.

'So finally I decided to open up a gallery. I had this beautiful space in Martello Street and I was struggling to articulate my own ideas. I still have a lot of ideas, and the shows that I choose for here are, in some ways, based around those ideas. We painted the floor grey and cleaned it up a little bit. The first show was David Troostwyk, a sound piece, and we made up a press release and sent it out and that was it. I didn't expect it to last very long.'

And so Matt's Gallery was born. Named after Klassnik's long since departed sheepdog, the gallery 'just sort of took off,' he recalls. Dedicated to the notion that the gallery should be a place

in which work can be tested and modified by the artist, Matt's Gallery adopted a policy that allowed for precisely that, rotating only three or four shows in a given year, with several months of run up time preceding an exhibit which might only last for a week or two. Early shows in the first years of the space included artists such as Joel Fisher, Susan Hiller, Tony Bevan, Amikam Toren and Klassnik's colleague, Kozlowski. But Klassnik insists the space was not about showing friends. 'I had a lot of friends who were artists, I was part of a community, but I didn't feel like I had any responsibility to them. I've shown very few friends – I've made a lot of friends through shows, though.'

If Matt's Gallery was not about hanging shows to placate pals, neither was it about cold, hard commercial decision making. 'I never wanted to sell work,' stresses Klassnik. 'I've always said that everything is potentially for sale, but I've never gone out to try and sell work. I didn't know how to do it and didn't feel comfortable with it. Look, I didn't really envision any of this when I started. I never really thought about how I was going to approach it, how long it was going to last, but I was serious from the word 'go'. What I wanted to do was show a piece of art as best I could, under the best possible conditions, so it was possible for the viewer to stand there and for him or her to be in an almost kind of privileged situation.

'In terms of the gallery (as an ongoing concern), I think it probably started occurring to me when everyone kept asking when I was going to move to Bond Street,' he continues. 'It was then that I realised I enjoyed them having to come to me, having difficulty getting to me – that was actually very important to my notion of the gallery. Martello Street was very difficult – you had to go into a studio complex, ring a bell and then three minutes later I would come down and open the door for you. You had to want to be there: every person was let in and let out. Once you got in you couldn't leave. It was like literally having a captive audience. It was quite friendly, though, and for a lot of shows which could be quite difficult to understand, viewers were given more time, which I liked. This idea of time – time spent getting to a place, time spent once you're there – is very important to me. This space is much the same thing, although it's about ten times easier to get to than Martello Street.'

Despite the relative isolation of the gallery's current Copperfield Road site, Klassnik increasingly finds himself included in a collection of galleries (Chisenhale, The Showroom, Interim) which, along with the well-established artists' community of the East End, has provoked a level of press interest in the area as London's 'new' centre for contemporary visual arts.

'It's an absolute red herring,' Klassnik says of such media generalisation. 'Since the mid-80s you've been reading about this centre. There are a lot of artists, but there always have been. Ever since we've been here, it's always 'The East End galleries are really happening,' but they never do. It's totally unimportant for me to be associated with Chisenhale, etc. They're just far enough away, as far as I'm concerned. I'd be worried if they were

any closer – there's just enough distance between them for people to turn off one space and then get ready for the other. Like in Foley Street, for example, you pop in and out of Karsten (Schubert), (Marc) Jancou, Laure Genillard and then down to Gilmour and then you wonder, "Where the hell have I been?" The idea of focus is important: You must come here and focus. At one time there was this idea of all of us getting together like New York, but that would not suit me.'

As time passed at Martello Street, it became clear that the rough-and-ready space was developing into a established gallery. Shows in the early and mid-80s included artists like Ian McKeever, Nan Hoover, Rose Finn-Kelcey, Ian Breakwell, Hannah Collins, Avis Newman and Richard Wilson. Artists were beginning to submit materials for Klassnik's perusal. 'I went out of my way to say please do not send things. I really didn't want people to submit unsolicited stuff – I didn't have a system to deal with it – but I did get around to see a lot of shows and met people that way. Richard Wilson came to me that way. He came up to me at a Serpentine show, Avis Newman's, and asked if I would come to his studio. I didn't know who he was, but I went and he had this little plan of Matt's Gallery he'd already made-up to show how things would work in the space. I found over the years that lots of people had little plans of the gallery made-up.' Wilson would go on to install some of the most memorable and famous works in the gallery's long history, including his reconstructive *She Came in Through The Bathroom Window* (1989), in which he repositioned an exterior window in the gallery space; *20:50* (1987), the remarkable sculptural installation using sump oil familiar to most from its long-term installation at the Saatchi Gallery in London, and *watertable* (1994), in which Wilson inaugurated the newly poured concrete floor by digging a hole in it down to the level of the local watertable and lowering a full size billiard table into it. These kinds of monumentally renovative projects are precisely what Klassnik must have hoped for when he started the gallery; putting a premium on development and allowing the artist the flexibility to try something in the space that they might not be able to do elsewhere. As Wilson himself said in an interview, 'On the three occasions since 1985 when I have worked and shown in the space, his commitment has verged on the fanatical.'

The Gallery continued its pace throughout the middle and late-80s, mounting shows by artists including Brian Catling, Jeff Instone, Kate Smith, Jimmie Durham, Edgar Heap of Birds and Melanie Counsell. During this time, the gallery was living from hand to mouth, with shows done mostly on funding from Klassnik and the artists, as well as a small but vital yearly amount from Greater London Arts (GLA), now the London Arts Board (LAB). But as the gallery prepared to enter its second decade in operation, Klassnik says it started to become clear that something had to change.

'It became clear that we needed more space,' he says of the decision to relocate. 'The space was closed more than it was open. The landlord started hassling us – this was 1990 – and we

and GLA had started a feasibility study of having a new space. I wanted to be paid and to give up teaching. I probably stayed in Martello Street longer than I should have, but we spent quite a long time looking for a new building. We wanted to find one that would be large enough and feel right, and with our resources that pretty much meant it had to be in the South or the East. I never wished for a posh West End space. We finally found this one and fell in love with it immediately. It was two buildings, just an empty warehouse. Every wall, every light, every floor, every door – everything – we did. I liked the location, especially the canal and I like the idea of getting here, and it's all sort of mucky and there's not much going on, and you get the feeling that maybe you've made the wrong turn, and then you open the door and walk in and you could be anywhere in the world. I like this idea of the "white cube" – it could be anywhere and you enter it and, like Alice, you're transformed.'

If the gallery can be said to transform those who enter it, it is also probably fair to say that Matt's Gallery has had some transformative effect on what has gone on around it, as well. Klassnik's dissatisfaction with the art world establishment of the late-70s found parallels a decade later with the emergence of the current generation of young British artists and their self-confident, pioneering spirit. The now-legendary alternative venue, DIY art shows of the late-80s – 'Modern Medicine', 'East Country Yard Show', 'Gambler' and especially Damien Hirst's 'Freeze' – provide the background against which today's maturing British art scene can be contextualised. Similarly, the experiment upon which Klassnik's embarked in 1979 provides a kind of presaging case study for today's full-blown phenomena, the macrocosmic evolutions of today's scene played out through the microcosm of Matt's Gallery.

'I wouldn't say that Matt's Gallery presaged what's going on in today's scene, but I suppose *one* could say that,' Klassnik diplomatically allows. 'It is true that artists have taken, like I did, the idea of showing into their own hands. The very existence of Matt's Gallery made it fairly obvious that you could show art and get an audience for it. I suppose it really did start (in the 80s) with Damien Hirst and "Freeze", but the reasons for doing it were very different. I think in some ways, while they've done very well for themselves in some respects, the artists creating the scene and this market for themselves can be a bit dangerous, too. A lot of people will have their 15 minutes, or 15 seconds, and then what? They probably have terrified (Nicholas) Logsdail (director of Lisson Gallery) and (Anthony) d'Offay, but most of these artists were dying to get into D'Offay and Lisson.

'The other thing about these shows that happen in warehouses,' Klassnik continues, 'Matt's is stationary, it has history, one show follows another. The old Matt's Gallery was small and people couldn't believe it was the same space show after show. There was a history of the space, not necessarily the surroundings but the actual history of what had been in there. For me, the interesting thing is the relationship between the artist and the container, the artist operating within the space. With the warehouse (shows), nine times out of ten the building is more interesting than the work. I don't object to artists making work specific to a place, but this idea of getting strange spaces to have artists work in seems to be just about some romantic idea of the broken down building site, tunnel or toilet.

'I don't necessarily think artists should have to find spaces, clean them up, act as gallery directors and make the work – I'm not sure that's the ideal thing for artists to be doing. Sometimes the shows can be quite interesting; the kind of place where you're not sure who made what until the end of the line where you get a piece of paper explaining it. You know, I quite like the concept of them putting it all together, but again the quality of the work has in certain cases not been too strong. (In that kind of setting) you can hide a lot of things.'

There is no room to hide in the austere 'white cube' interior of Matt's Gallery's current space in Copperfield Road, and there have been a variety of responses to the intrinsic details of the location, in the work that Kate Smith, David Troostwyk, Willie Doherty, Thomas Holley, Richard Wilson and Mel Jackson have executed there over the last 18 months. 'I offer a space, a container,' says Klassnik. 'What the artist puts in it is up to them. I've always seen the gallery's job as providing a space for the artist to make a work basically for him, or her, and me, and then inviting other people in to see it. That strategy hasn't changed because we've moved; it's just more space, and, I suppose, artists have become more ambitious since I've been here. I mean, I remember being at the old space with less money and while there was ambition there, we could always do it. There's a kind of grandeur that's developed here, and that's OK as long as you can sustain it. My rent used to be nothing, now it's £28,500. Before, I could paint the floor myself the night before with a couple of gallons of Dulux; now it's 200 quids worth of Dulux and a two-day job. I used to work in the space with the artists; on the show that's going up right now, there are three other guys in there working on the installation.'

The growth and development of the space has made some degree of letting go necessary for Klassnik, who is still intimately involved with the day-to-day operations of the gallery, having only one other full-time person, administrator Alison Raftery, whose skills Klassnik praises as central to the smooth running of the space just as he admits to having a difficult time with delegating responsibility even to her. Yet because Matt's Gallery has always been more than just a functional expression – incorporating as it does so much of Klassnik's own artistic sensibility, in effect, one long-term, ongoing conceptual gesture – Klassnik has more than a simple workaday relationship to its progress. 'I am concerned about (having to let go),' he says. 'I don't want an enormous staff – if things got too far out of control I would probably just close. I have been able to give away a little bit, though: I remember when it was very important for me to wash the floor myself.'

Has the gallery prevented him from exploring his own work more fully? 'This is the work,' Klassnik emphasises. 'Has it derailed me from doing something else? Where would I start? I wouldn't know how to begin. I made this choice before I opened the space. I see so many of my ideas in the two spaces over the years – not in all cases, but almost everything I see here is in some way related to a concept that I might have had. This is my artistic endeavour, this is the way I've decided to be an artist. It's no different from directing or producing in a theatre where you take on different people.'

This notion of the curatorial gesture being itself artistic is of particular significance in contemporary aesthetic discourse, with the current renaissance of the curator/*auteur* and the phenomena, again presaged by Klassnik, of the artist-become-curator, locally manifested by people like Hirst, first in the context of 'Freeze', but more recently and in a more fully realised sense, in his 'Some Went Mad . . . ' exhibition, which toured from 1994-95 in the US.

So, are all curatorial efforts artistic, or is there something unique about Matt's Gallery that makes it feel that way? 'I think there is something special about the way we work,' says Klassnik. 'The artist is in the space working from anything up to three months and I'm in the space as well nearly everyday and we discuss things. Over the years, one can actually see various bits that may be more Robin than anything else – the level of collaboration differs from artist to artist. It's not a democracy; I'm not into democracy – but I worry about every show in the same way that an artist worries. I feel truly responsible, much more so than if I had just been programming a space for 15 years.'

Despite the fact that the 48 year old Klassnik has already devoted a third of his life to Matt's Gallery, his long-term plans for the space remain open. 'I haven't set any time on it. I have a 15 year lease on this building, so I'll be nearly 65 when it's done. Then the gallery will probably go away – I can't see how it could continue. I don't see it as a family business. It has, though, opened up possibilities for others to use it as a model, I think. I have a sense that others may have taken something away from it.'

One of the most interesting symptoms of these 15 years for the gallery and the consistent growth it's managed to sustain over that time, is a sense of creeping venerability. Is there a feeling that what started out as an oppositional gesture towards the Establishment has, like so many other things before it, with time become firmly 'established' itself? 'I'm very conscious of the fact that, by virtue of longevity, I've become part of the Establishment. I'm also very conscious of the fact that tomorrow evening, for instance, I'll sit with 200 people at the Tate's Turner Prize dinner. (Willie Doherty, an artist who has shown regularly at Matt's Gallery since the beginning of the 90s was short-listed for the 1994 prize, ultimately won by Antony Gormley). But I'm not going to be there because of the kind of person I am or my lifestyle. I'm there for one reason only – because the artist happens to be showing a piece of work that comes from here. I'd not be sitting there otherwise.'

From an interview with Robin Klassnik – 21st November 1994

Jeffrey Kastner is a writer and critic. Recently relocated from the UK to Boston, he is a former London Correspondent for ARTnews *and is currently US Editor of* Art Monthly. *He is a frequent contributor to newspapers and magazines in the US and Europe, and his work has appeared in publications including* Artforum, ARTnews, Flash Art *and* Frieze.

PAGE 28: David Troostwyk, detail from Trophy on Velvet; *PAGE 30: Thomas Holley, detail; PAGE 32: Kate Smith, detail from* Levitation; *PAGES 35-37: Mel Jackson, . . . do you or have you ever?, 1994, glass tubing, liquid, leather-covered tables, pump, lights, TV and video; PAGES 38-39: David Troostwyk; RIGHT:* War Memorial, *1994, 16.7 x 243.7cm; LEFT:* Couch: Previously owned by Sigmund Freud, *1994, 183 x 184cm, both resin/black pigment on white primed canvas; PAGE 40-41: Thomas Holley, 1994, sandblasted glass, black and white photograph and lenses; PAGE 42-43: Kate Smith, 1993; PAGE 44-45: Willie Doherty,* The Only Good One is a Dead One, *1993, double screen video projection with sound; PAGE 46-47: Richard Wilson,* watertable, *1994, full size billiard table, concrete pipe, groundwater and electrics. Photos Stephen White and Edward Woodman.*

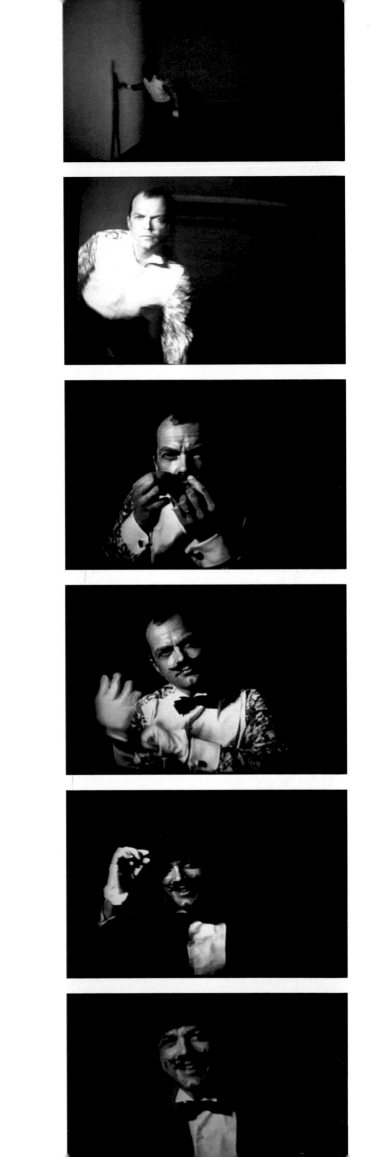

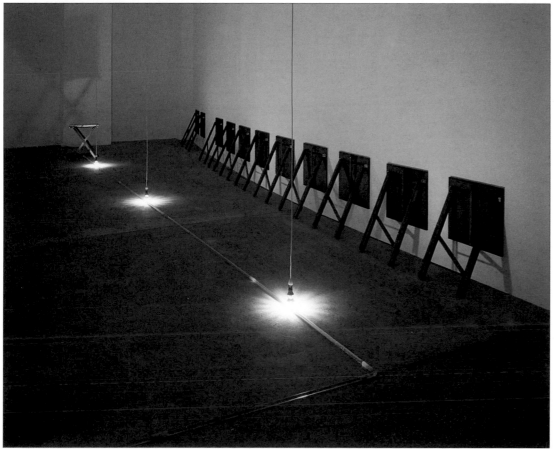

MEL JACKSON

. . . do you or have you ever? 1994

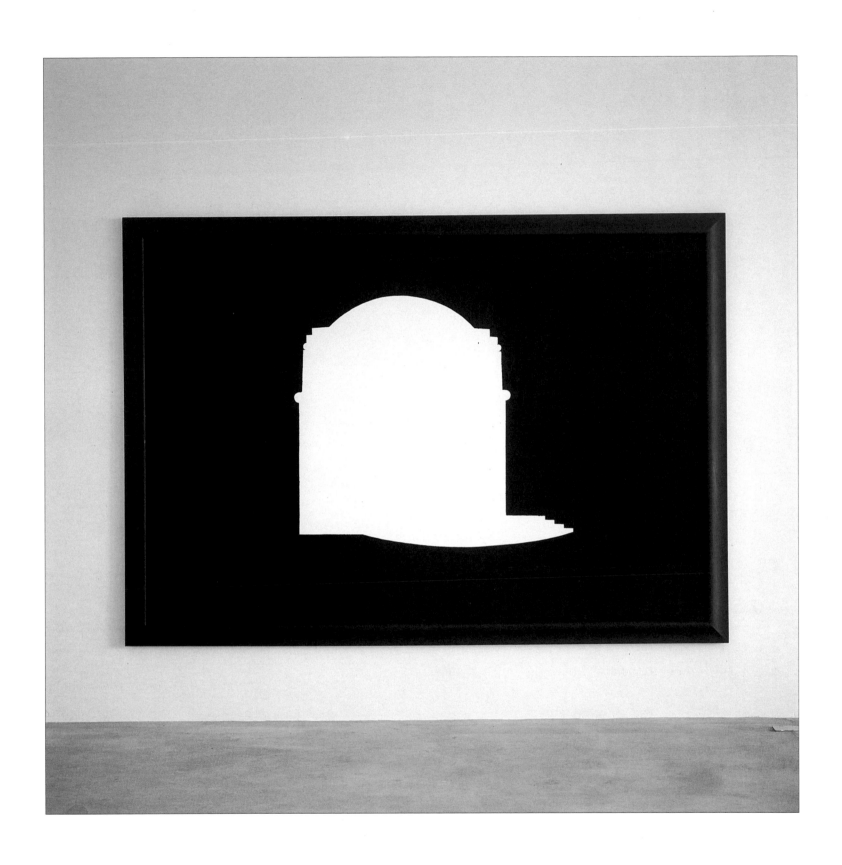

DAVID TROOSTWYK

1994

THOMAS HOLLEY

1994

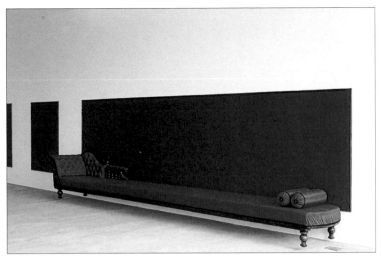

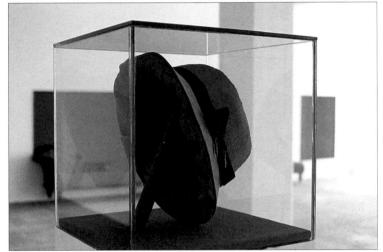

KATE SMITH

1993

As my assassin jumps out in front of me everything starts to happen in slow motion. I can see him raise his gun and I can't do a thing. I see the same scene shot from different angles. I see a sequence of fast edits as the car swerves to avoid him and he starts shooting. The windscreen explodes around me. I see a clump of dark green bushes in front of me, illuminated by the car headlights. The car crashes out of control and I feel a deep burning sensation in my chest.

It might be just as easy on the street. I could wait until he's coming out of the house or I could just walk up to the door, ring the bell and when he answers, BANG BANG! Let the fucker have it.

It should be an easy job with a car waiting at the end of the street. I've seen it so many times I could write the script.

WILLIE DOHERTY

The Only Good One is a Dead One 1993

RICHARD WILSON

watertable 1994

Maud Sulter, Quelques Instants Plus Tard, Monique Cherchait Sa Brosse À Cheveux, *1993, (Hélas l'Héroïne series of three) photographic print, matt laminate, mount, raw oak frame, 101.6 x 76.2cm*

EDDIE CHAMBERS
AN INTERVIEW WITH PETRINE ARCHER-STRAW

Petrine Archer-Straw – *Eddie, you have a reputation, as both a radical black artist and a radical black curator. In fact, in your most recent catalogues you have employed the slogan 'No art but Black art. No war but Class War.' Could you expand on this?*
Eddie Chambers – Well, I think the 'No war but Class War' part is probably self-evident, or self-explanatory. In terms of 'No art but Black art,' what I'm trying to say is what I've been saying for a number of years now: that the only kind of art that is important in the black community, is art that focuses on the black struggle and sees itself as an integral part of our struggle against racism. So really the slogan is a summary of the idea that our art should have a politicised agenda.

You suggest that 'No war but Class War' is fairly self-evident, but surely that links the black community and black art within a larger framework of revolutionary struggle.
– Yes, it does. That's true, I can't really add anything else to what you've said, it does add a class dimension to our struggle.

Your term also suggests that black art must be prioritised. How do you go about doing that in your curatorial practice?
– In terms of the exhibitions I curate, I'm always trying to seek out artists, who I think, address that call for a politicised art form. So that's my starting point, seeking out artists whose works address the black experience and black concerns. Then, the focus shifts to how I can find an outlet for that work. There is an issue here regarding a process of alienation, between the black community and black artists, which has not yet been fully addressed.

Yes, I realise you're doing a lot of work especially in regions where there are black communities, has this been something that you've done from choice, or is it because you've had difficulties getting black art accepted in mainstream London institutions?
– I have to say that I think, in the years I've been curating, my ability to get shows within London has been abysmal. I mean, obviously there are a few exceptions – it's not been a wholly bleak picture – but it has been very difficult to get shows within London. Generally speaking, it's been much easier to get shows in the north of England. The area between West Midlands and the North East, has been the region which has been most receptive to my work.

I think it's very difficult to see any aspect of what I do as being free from tensions and contradictions. I think there are a number of different issues inherent in exhibiting black art. Certain galleries have a notion that they don't need black exhibitions because they don't have a large enough black community in the area to merit it. I don't think it's acceptable for a gallery to say that. On the other hand, when galleries situated in regions with a large black community do have black exhibitions, it probably suits an ultimately racist agenda, in terms of fulfilling a token slot. I have a lot of problems with tokenism, as if the provision of one or two specifically black shelves somehow addresses the needs and the concerns of the black community. On one level I'm really pleased with increasing opportunities to exhibit, but on another level I don't think the motives are always acceptable. So I think these tensions and difficulties, resulting from art world racism in various forms, are never far from my work.

You've actually had a successful record of exhibitions in the past five years or so. How long have you been practising as a curator?
– I began organising exhibitions in 1981, and I started to curate exhibitions in 1987. I make a distinction between organising and curating, in that when I was organising exhibitions, from the early to mid-80s, it was a case of showing a group of young black artists and art students, and I included my own work in that. It was round about 1986-87 that I made a conscious choice to move from having an active involvement in the exhibitions, to being somebody who curated.

And through this curatorial practice, do you have your own agenda, in terms of the issues that need to be addressed?
– Oh, very much so. Again, there are difficulties there that I'm aware of, because I believe the artist's concerns and priorities have to come first, but in a way I set the agenda, in the way I construct my exhibitions, especially ones that have a very strong subject matter. For example, the exhibition about the British flag[1] that I did in 1993, that was wholly my construction, and obviously there was a lot of work which reinforced and supported the arguments I was putting forward. Essentially, it's an interventionist role for a curator, it's not just in response to what's out there. There's also an element of commissioning work, for instance, asking an artist to make work about the Union Jack rather than just making a selection from work that already exists.

And what are the major themes that your curatorial work has addressed in the past? You've mentioned the 'Black People and the British Flag' exhibition. What else have you felt needed to be addressed urgently?

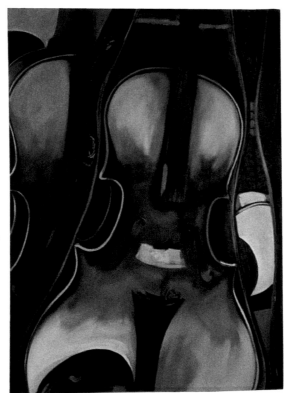

Eugene Palmer, ABOVE: In The Garden *(diptych), oil on canvas, 288 x 160cm; BELOW:* Southern News *(diptych), 1990, oil on canvas, 289.56 x 152.4cm*

– Well, in 1994 I did an exhibition called 'Us and Dem'[2], which was an exhibition that attempted to explore some of the relationships between the black community and the police, because I think the issue of the black community's relationship with the police, the judiciary and the criminal justice system is of critical importance. And I was interested in focusing on the work of a number of artists whose work, I thought, addressed those issues. Another exhibition, which I worked on awhile ago, was 'History and Identity'[3], because I think the notion of history, and the notion of identity, are really central to the work of a lot of black artists. I mean, obviously it's also important to a lot of other artists as well, but I think specifically for us, identity is a critical issue, and it's reinforced wherever in the world we are. I think it's separate from the idea of racism. Obviously, racism informs the issue of identity, but it goes way beyond the issues of racism and discrimination. Identity is a constant friction within our minds.

You've also done a series of one person exhibitions. What informed your choice of those artists?
– I think the starting point for the one person shows I've worked on has been artists whose subject matter has embraced the black experience, embraced notions of black identity. And in that sense, Eugene Palmer and Michael Platt are excellent examples. As I say, my agenda has always been to encourage the establishment of an art form that clearly addresses the black experience. Now, obviously, artists like Platt and Palmer are not just seen in terms of being black artists, they're seen as being artists in a much wider, freer sense, but their work does address specific aspects of the black experience, and it's that that interests me.

Yes, Platt, – an African American artist whose work you showed here in Britain for the first time in 1994 – that illustrates that you're also interested in the black experience elsewhere, and not just centred on black British artists.
– Yes, absolutely. I'm always hesitant to pin a clear label on myself in terms of my ideas, in terms of politics, but if I have to, I'd say my ideas focus on Pan-Africanism. I would call myself a Pan-Africanist if I had to call myself anything, because I believe that people of African descent, spread throughout our diaspora, are linked. There are many things which we have in common.

Historically and culturally?
– Yes, historically, culturally and in terms of the contemporary experience. So it's for those reasons that I was quite keen to see artists from other parts of the black diaspora exhibited here; and similarly I've also had an interest in getting the work of British based black artists pushed out further afield. On the subject of Pan-Africanism, I feel very strongly that in Britain we have a body of black artists which, in the international sense, is very astutely aware of their international identity, or the international aspect of their identity. And having been to a number of places in the US

and Europe and so on, and seen the work of black artists, I don't think there's anything quite like the body of work there is here, in terms of its ability to address a wider community. If you look at the work of Keith Piper, Eugene Palmer and a number of other people, you will see international references, in terms of African communities, that you just won't find in other parts of the world. I know that's something you might argue with or disagree with.

I would argue that for any artist, be they black or white, there will always be a kind of cross-referencing internationally, and certainly, modern art practice is premised upon a type of cultural exchange within the work.
Yes, but I'm not talking about that so much – I'm talking about clear references to our political history . . .

A common history?
– Yes. For example, there are artists in Britain whose work has dealt with the issue of lynching in the US, and although it may exist, I have not yet seen a body of work by an artist in the US that addresses the British experience. When I was growing up, working with Keith Piper, Donald Rodney and those people, we were doing work on South Africa, anti-apartheid work, and we were taking our cues largely from the Black Power struggle in the US. The work was incredibly internationalist. I mean, if anything there was a problem in that it didn't sufficiently address the black experience in Britain. And I haven't seen an equivalent body of work around the world. I think other people's concerns are much more localised. I'm not saying that's a problem, but I do think in Britain we have a unique grasp of Pan-Africanism; it's a very vigorous and very alive issue.

You mentioned this early group of young black artists who were working together, again through a series of exhibitions which in the 80s were called 'The Pan-Afrikan Connection'. What has happened to that early group?
– Well, we disbanded in early 1984, and since then we've kind of gone our separate ways.

The reason I enquired was to elicit what kind of changes might have taken place for young black artists who were initially exhibiting during the 80s. I wonder if they have been forced, or coerced, into abandoning their role as practising black artists, and whether, because of circumstances, they have had to take on other roles within the art community. If this is true, was it linked in any way to the influence of the 80s economy or other related phenomena?
– I think there's been a real problem in terms of artists who abandon their practice. There are a number of artists who I think have been lost to the black community, because they've abandoned their practice in favour of desk-bound jobs, whether in the visual arts or otherwise. I don't think it's something which affects us to a disproportionate degree. When I was at art school, there

were probably 50 people in my year who graduated; I would be surprised if any more than two or three of those people maintain their practice in a consistent way. Obviously, there are people who become Sunday painters – I'm not saying that in a disparaging way – but you know, I don't think it's a problem which has a disproportionate effect on black people.

Well, then, what have the problems been for black artists in the 80s and 90s, if any?
– I think the biggest problem has been the racism of the art world and how it manifests itself; as a general umbrella problem. At the beginning of the 80s, black artists in Britain were a generic mass. If you like, they were kind of lumpen body. By 1986-87, four or five artists broke away from the pack, and those artists were deemed to be our 'best' artists. Since then, I think the problem for the mass of black artists has been a lack of exhibition opportunities which have been hogged by a mere handful of artists. I know that's a dreadful thing to say, but it's such a frustrating situation. Obviously I think it's in the nature of the artist to accept and seek opportunities to exhibit, but I think the reality is that, as a result, a large body of gifted black artists have been ignored.

Can we concentrate for a moment on the few that have actually made it, or are attempting to make it in the British art scene? On what grounds do you think they are successful?
– Well, I think the art world sees their work has having a sophistication and a richness that they approve of, or can relate to. I think these artists are seen as being OK because they're deemed to be highly visually literate.

Could we have some names? I mean, who would you suggest is successful now as a black artist?
– In terms of the African-Caribbean community of artists, I'd say, since the mid-80s, I think Keith Piper has probably been one of the most successful male artists. I think, in terms of women artists, Maud Sulter has developed, in recent years, into a very important black artist, and Sonia Boyce, obviously, is somebody who is very familiar to a lot of people. I think the South Asian body of artists is slightly different, but there is a kind of corresponding body of artists from that particular community.

Do you think that British art institutions are looking for a particular type of imagery?
– Oh, absolutely, I think they're looking for something which is, as I say, sophisticated. But I also think the art Establishment is looking for people it can embrace as 'one of us', 'people who can speak our language', and I don't think most of our painters have been taken on board in that sort of way.

Since becoming a curator you've said that you feel you are being as creative in that field as you might have been as an artist.

Would you consider your curatorial role to be as influential, or more so, than when you were an artist?
– I believe my curatorial role has been more influential because, as you mentioned earlier, I do see myself as working for those black artists who have been somewhat marginalised. I think the act of trying to secure exhibition space for that body of artists who might not otherwise be exhibited, is very important to me. The scale of the marginalisation of these artists is massive. Particularly if we consider that many of them are only able to exhibit their work in exhibitions such as those I curate, or smaller efforts at a community level. I think there are major problems, and I don't think that the needs of these artists are being properly addressed at the moment.

That brings us to what you might perceive as being the failings of the British mainstream institutions in providing for black artists. How do you view the situation, in terms of funding and in terms of exhibiting space, and so on?
– I mean, I don't really want to take a kind of negative, pessimistic road, but I think that at the moment things are absolutely dreadful. (Laughter) I think, in the early 80s, there was this thing about 'Right, we've just had these amazing riots throughout the country,' and that translates, in its own kind of trickle-down way, into a pressure on public institutions, to have some kind of accountability, or to acknowledge in some way people in the black community and, in this case, artists in the black community. I think what's happened, is that the art world is now saying, 'Right, there are a few artists who we will patronise . . . who we'll interact with . . . that there is a multicultural body of artists out there.' Of course, the problem is that I don't think that the process of patronising half a dozen artists is adequate, because it means that there are several hundred artists in any one area of the country who are left to wither. I think it's a really important point that racism in the art world, in terms of denying exhibition spaces to black artists, is a real problem, because I think art practice improves or develops through exhibitions. I don't think an artist is going to improve or mature, or develop a high level of competence and accomplishment only in their studio. If you give an artist an opportunity to exhibit a major body of his or her work, then I think that process acts as a catalyst for that artist's work. So essentially, I don't like to say it, but I believe strongly that what we have in the black community is a body of artists whose work is actually stunted. I really hate to say that, but I believe it strongly.

And do you feel that this sort of stunting process has taken place over the past decade or so, or has the situation always been the same for black artists in this country? I'm really questioning if the situation is improving or deteriorating.
– I think the situation is definitely not improving.

I question whether this idea of a standoff isn't an improvement.

– So are you saying it is an improvement?

I'm asking: isn't it an improvement? At least there's no active undermining of the black artists or . . .
– Well, it depends on what you mean by 'active'. I think the act of ignoring people is very active, or it has an active repercussion. I don't think what we have at the moment is acceptable, but I think there's not a great deal that we can do about it. However, I am very hesitant to continue curating in the kinds of ways I have been curating. I have increasing difficulties with this idea that I exist to curate black exhibitions in an otherwise white exhibition programme. For years I was happy to do that, because I saw myself in a kind of pioneering role, but as soon as you start to think that you're actually suiting someone else's agenda, in terms of black slots, then the whole thing becomes much more problematic.

I agree with you that exhibition exposure contributes to the development and maturity of an artist, and that the way in which their work is critiqued also helps artists to build confidence in what they have to say. I wonder if there is ever going to be a kind of way forward for black artists here, and if their circumstances aren't always going to remain limited by virtue of the problems that you've outlined.
– I think the notions of 'British art' and 'black artists' are ultimately incompatible. I say that because, in order for a notion of British art to percolate and to have a currency, there's an implication that there's a body of black artists who are operating on a level playing field with their white counterparts, essentially equal.

It's like art in Jamaica: obviously, some of the issues which we've touched on can be translated to a Jamaican context, but at the same time, the major positive difference is that there, artists are all operating from a similar kind of plateau, and it's from that plateau that their work can be assessed, in terms of its differences and its similarities. I don't think that the work of black artists in Britain is free enough to be included in a general notion of 'British art', in a fair and equal way.

Things have changed since the 80s, and we've had a lot of rhetoric with regard to the notion of British multiculturalism. Don't you see that as a way forward, in terms of how we assess these artists and how their work is reviewed and represented?
– Well, I think the major problems with institutional notions such as 'multiculturalism' and, I suppose most recently, 'internationalism', which is another area altogether . . .

Well, it isn't, surely it's an extension of the same principle.
– No, no, no. I mean . . . (Laughter)

You mean it's another minefield.
– Yes, that's another minefield. I think the problem with these notions is that, whilst we can embrace the spirit of them quite

easily and quite readily, the way they find form, via the white Establishment, is always through a quota system. I don't really think the white Establishment is able to take on board the spirit of multiculturalism in a truly unfettered way.

So is this the reason for your commitment to an agenda which, I suggest, is separatist?
– Speaking candidly, whilst I've always had an idealistic agenda in terms of forging ever stronger links between black artists and the black community, I don't think that there's a great deal of evidence that those links have been adequately forged.

But how, Eddie, can you suggest that you ought to be pursuing this independent agenda of promoting black British art, and to some extent promoting it exclusively, but through the agency of British exhibition institutions, with British institutional funding? Don't you think that you're biting the hand that feeds you?
– I don't really feel I'm biting the hand that feeds me or anything like that, because I think British funding bodies have an obligation – though obviously I can't compel them to fund me or other black artists – to allocate funding to black artists in Britain. I think galleries should be pressed to show a wider body of artists than they do. I think you can ask me, in all fairness and in all honesty: 'is that sufficiently a priority? Shouldn't my priority be addressing the black community itself?' You could ask me that, and I would accept that as a valid question. But if you ask me that, then in some ways that leaves this whole other flank regarding institutional funding unaddressed.

Obviously you take a position which is agitational rather than one of a mediator. Do you think that there's any value to taking a more passive approach to dealing with British art institutions? Do you think that more might be achieved by using a lighter touch?
– No, I don't. I mean, I despair about the negative tone of our conversation, in parts. I think it's something which causes us both . . .

Concern?
– Concern and discomfort. I know that to talk primarily in terms of 'race' is often crude and vulgar, but you know, there is absolutely no evidence that any black person in the art world is ever going to be taken seriously in terms of their abilities. I don't think there's any evidence that a more cautious, mediating or hesitant position is going to reap any more rewards.

Can I ask you what might seem to be a more fundamental question, based on my perceptions of what actually takes place here in Britain. My feeling has always been that there has been a preoccupation, a preponderance of interest in race as an issue, and a lot of energy is diverted into a perceived struggle with British art institutions. By contrast, in other countries, in black countries, artists obviously get on with their work and they don't

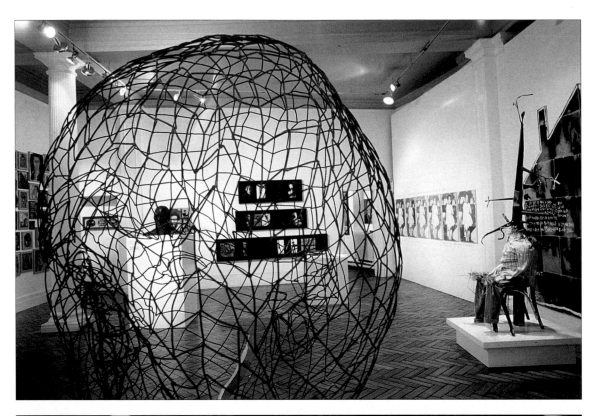

ABOVE: (left) Permindar Kaur, Self Portrait, *1990, (right) Donald Rodney,* The House that Jack Built, *1990, from 'Let The Canvas Come To Life With Dark Faces', 1990, Bluecoat Gallery Liverpool;*
BELOW: Veena Stephenson, ring a ring a roses, *1992, mixed media, 210 x 150 x 90cm, from 'Black People and The British Flag', 1993, Cornerhouse, Manchester and the City Gallery, Leicester*

have to tackle issues of identity in the same sort of confrontational way. Do you think that there's a way forward by deflating the black issue, the notion of a black aesthetic and the problems that are inherent in taking such a clear-cut separatist stance?

– I understand the question you're asking, and I'm glad you've asked it. In response to it, I think that, whilst on the one hand there's been a black presence in Britain for hundreds of years, on the other hand our generation of black people have only been here for a limited period. I think we're in an evolutionary process, and I think five or ten years down the line we could have a completely different situation vis-à-vis the work of black artists and British art. When I meet artists who've graduated in the past couple of years or so, although I can see in their work a very distinct black subject matter, their concerns and a lot of their sensibilities are completely different from mine.

Yes, I'm asking is there any benefit to that type of evolution, where one moves away from separatist issues into something more collective, more international, more Post-Modern even?

– Essentially what we're talking about is a process of assimilation, don't you think?

And is there benefit to that?

– I'm not sure we can see it in terms of benefits or lack of benefits. I just think it's an inevitable process, although I also think assimilation brings with it a technical estrangement from our countries of origin.

And you don't wish to see that, obviously, as a Pan-Africanist?

– Well, I don't, but technically, people born in the 70s or even the early 80s, I think for them, even 'Jamaica', or the 'Caribbean', are going to be removed entities. Because in a sense, my own bridge to Jamaica is my parents.

It's a relatively strong one, I imagine.

– Yes, I know that my parents were born in Jamaica, I know where they were born in Jamaica, I know that that's where they're from. Now, if you look at children born in Basildon, Rotherham or wherever, in 1972 or 1981, that connection with Jamaica, Nigeria, Ghana, or wherever, becomes more and more tenuous.

Yes, and by the same token, they then have to make their investments here in this country.

– Exactly.

Also, they have to stake a claim for their creativity in this country and through the institutions of this country. To what extent should that claim be based on old notions which are separatist, as opposed to a new way of looking at identity which is . . .

– I will never stop believing that artists have an obligation to address and to bear in mind the political realities of the communities that produce them. I will never encourage artists to turn their backs on direct dialogues with their communities. What you're suggesting is that in order to move forward, artists need to turn their backs on the political realities of what's happening to their brothers, their sisters, their cousins, their uncles, and so on and so forth. Unfortunately, by virtue of being involved in the arts, there is an inevitable estrangement from the black community. However, I think black artists cannot afford to forget our communities, we can't forget those realities. We can't forget police brutality, we can't forget deaths in police custody. I don't think we could pursue a kind of Post-Modernist dream at the expense of what's happening to our people.

We've assumed that we're using the term 'black art' in a way which is clearly understood, but I know that in the early 80s the problem of definition, and how one defined black art, was one which plagued you, particularly around an exhibition like 'Plotting the Course'[4]. I wonder if, ten years on, the notion of black art is any more clearly defined?

– In the early 80s, my working definition of black art was that it was art by black people, for black people, about black people and that it was art that specifically addressed the black experience, the political conditions and so on and so forth. Some of that I think we've touched on previously, and my thinking was very much that by 'black' I was referring to people of African origin – African-Caribbean and African origin. Now, I haven't really ever stopped thinking that that is the only plausible definition of 'black', and all the exhibitions I worked on between 1981 and 1987 were of African and Caribbean artists. By the time it got down to 'Plotting the Course', which was in 1988, I think what happened was that I was kind of overwhelmed, steamrollered by this other view that 'black' should include all sorts of other people beyond the African diaspora.

Now this other view was one which had developed out of a kind of a multicultural debate.

– That's right, yes. This was the view that 'black' had to embrace, or should embrace, people beyond the African diaspora. Although, I've never really stopped believing that 'black' is really a term that belongs exclusively to us as African people.

People of African descent?

– People of African origin. But I have to say that the multicultural definition of 'black', as it snowballed throughout the 80s, has been quite considerable. So much so, that now, even though I have to do an 'oral-double' take, I think a lot of my practice has reflected that.

Well, certainly in exhibitions that you've curated, you have gone out of your way to ensure that people of other racial origins have been included.

– That's right. But the shows that you're talking about, Petrine – shows such as 'Plotting the Course' and my self-portrait show,[5] –

Keith Piper, Surveillances: Tagging the Other, *1992, still from computer animation*

were exhibitions where publicity material was sent out, I think quite widely, and it was up to the artists to respond to what they saw in this blurb. It was the artists' choice as to whether they wanted to identify with what I was doing and my working definitions of the term black.

Are you not selective in your curatorial practice now, don't you pinpoint the artists that you wish to work with?
– Yes, but I like to think my practice has matured, that I've moved on considerably from those early, quite cumbersome exhibitions, to exhibitions such as the Michael Platt exhibition, the Eugene Palmer retrospective. I like to think that these have been much more considered and focused exhibitions.

Yes, but do you think that you'd say the same for your art practice? I know that your output is more limited now that you are curating, but you do exhibit occasionally. Would you say that you would see the same process of maturation taking place in how you communicate black issues through your work?
– I would like to think so, but I'm hesitant to say that, because I think what you're really talking about is a process of dilution. I think that's what has happened to the work of a lot of black British artists in the 80s. I don't think it's a maturing process.

It's an accommodating one.
– Yes, I think it's a process of compromise; I think it's a process of work being toned down to suit 'other' palates, 'other' tastes. And I don't like the idea that my practice may have undergone that transition.

Dr Petrine Archer-Straw is a Jamaican Art Historian and is currently lecturing at the Courtauld Institute of Art in London, she is also a freelance curator and writer.

Eddie Chambers was born in Wolverhampton in 1960. He began organising exhibitions with a group of Black art students, including Keith Piper, in 1980. He has since curated a large number of exhibitions of work by Black artists in Britain and abroad. In 1989 he established the African and Asian Visual Artist's Archive, a Black artists' research and reference facility. He has also written extensively on the subject of Black visual art practice. Eddie Chambers lives in Bristol.

Notes

1 'Black People and the British Flag', The Corner House, Manchester, 1993; The City Gallery, Leicester, 1993.
2 'Us and Dem', The Storey Institute, Lancaster, 1994.
3 'History and Identity', The Norwich Gallery, Norwich, 1991.
4 'Black Art Plotting the Course', Oldham Art Gallery, Oldham, and touring, 1988.
5 'Let the Canvas Come to Life With Dark Faces', Coventry Herbert Art Gallery and Museum, Coventry, and touring, 1990.

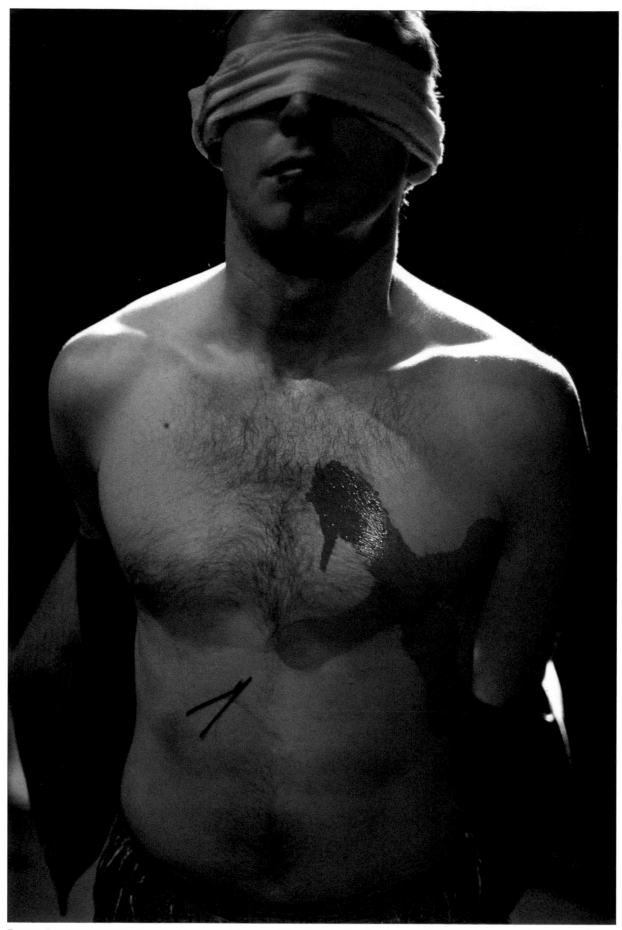

Forced Entertainment make performance work for a variety of contexts – theatres, galleries and unusual sites. Formed in 1984 the company are one of the UK's most acclaimed and long-lived performance ensembles, inspiring other groups and artists with their explorations of Urban Experience, the media culture and issues of contemporary identity. Tim Etchells has written text for all of the group's projects and has directed the work since 1986. Above: Hidden J (photo Hugo Glendinning)

PERFORMING QUESTIONS
FORCED ENTERTAINMENT, DESPERATE OPTIMISTS, RECKLESS SLEEPERS AND BLAST THEORY
An Interview With Adrian Heathfield

The presence and tenacity of Live Art practices in a culture driven by reproduction and commodification seems strangely anachronistic. Though we certainly consume live events, they quickly disperse into the ether of the individual's consciousness; they resist and elude our desire to name, record and own them. Yet, in Britain today there is a vibrant and expanding Live Art scene, increasingly sustained through experimentation at the crossed margins of forms, disciplines and cultural identities. The artists who speak in the following interview only reflect one aspect of this diverse constellation of hybrid makers; they work in the borderland where performance in real time and space comes to challenge and destabilise the verities and structures of theatrical representation.

Elsewhere in Europe, artists such as Wilson, Bausch and Anderson were declared the 'New Theatre Mainstream' and the dense diversity of forms which followed in their wake have been labelled the 'Post-Avant-Garde'. Applied to a British context these phrases seem sadly ridiculous as the theatre mainstream has resisted change with an institutional fortitude. By policing its borders, and sustaining exclusions, it has maintained its uniform mono-cultural outlook, from time to time conceding the odd minor assimilation. British theatre culture has remained largely ignorant of the performance Other, without and within, supported by a theatrical journalism so critically crusty as to be almost 'unrecyclable'.

The featured artists all create in a spirit of connection rather than isolation. Their work draws on diverse cultural forms as readily as performance art heritage and is primarily wedded to the exploration of contemporary experience. Since the early 80s performance-theatre has shed its aphasia and got seriously textual. This shift has been achieved without a return to textual authority and the centred subject speaking in a 'spontaneous' voice. Now text invariably appears as one element in a layered aesthetic composition, often with its mediating operations exposed. The emphases on indeterminacy, the evacuation of value, the impossibility of presence, which was so much a part of late-80s performance, has given way to a renewed interest in reformulating aesthetics around ethical and political concerns. As the differences of opinion in this interview show, the terms of this move are still in contestation.

Transient and hard to reproduce, the actual performances of which the artists speak evade determination by discourse. As a spectator, the performance archivist or theorist is also disabled in her quest to know the event; she is left reconstructing, sifting remnants and restaging memories, her attempts to transform the

work into intellectual property are undeniably marked by failure. How, then, to record or write on performance? What value can we attach to the artist's description of effect, let alone intention? Whose history will be written in the remainders of 90s Live Art? This document, amongst others, is a subjective and damaged trace.

Tim Etchells of Forced Entertainment discussing *Hidden J*.
Joe Lawlor of desperate optimists discussing *Hope*.
Mole Wetherell of Reckless Sleepers discussing *Parasite*.
Ju Row Farr/Matt Adams of Blast Theory discuss *Stampede*.

02:10:01

Adrian Heathfield – *There is a tradition in performance art of destabilising the work-as-product by making the performance evidently part of an ongoing process. How do you make a piece like* Hidden J, *and is it continually evolving*?
Tim Etchells – We work very slowly – exploring ideas for text, action, space, sound-track. For many months, in rehearsal, these elements are fluid, always changing, but there comes a point in the process when we recognise the essence and structure of the work that we are going to make. Once we are touring we like to have it pretty fixed. Occasionally we have wrecked a piece by continuing to tackle it when it should have been left as it was.

You find other ways to open the work and make it question itself? – In the final piece, the elements and textures are balanced – different fictions are placed next to each other not so much linked, as allowed to resonate in all their connection and disconnection. We make structures in which the elements challenge or comment on each other. So, in *Hidden J* Claire spends most of the time excluded from the action sitting with a sign that says 'liar' around her neck. Her presence quietly and continuously upsets the rest of the show. We are concerned with those moments, or forces, in a work which re-frame and ask questions of the performance material.

[words removed]

02:41:23

'What here is meant', 'what here is true, sincere, a stupid lie, a joke'? These are questions for a living and artistic practice where much of our time is spent saying words and performing actions in

Forced Entertainment, ABOVE: Hidden J; *BELOW:* Club of No Regrets, *(photos Hugo Glendinning)*

front of groups of strangers. What is the truth or essence of that situation, what do they want to see us do and what do we need to do in front of them? The biggest question I ask of performance work is 'does it feel as if the people on stage are in danger', not in some glib professional way, but in an actual way, somehow exposing themselves. I look for moments when performers are bound up in a struggle, perhaps implicated in some on-stage power relationship, and through that connected to wider questions of power.

01:27:00

Joe Lawlor – It's not a hideous notion to imagine that a company could make just one performance; a piece so fluid in its structure that it could encompass its own destruction; a piece made of endless transmutations. We have found that if you constantly unsettle what the performers are doing, they never get to a point where they have authorship within the work. That sense of ownership is important. It's only through feeling in control that the performers begin to uncover new areas.

Richard Foreman talks about truth leaping and stumbling across the stage. As makers we are always trying to go beyond ourselves again and trying to create a space for truth; the difficulty is recognising, and knowing it, when it does happen. Because of the delicacy of truth you can't place it in a piece, all you can do is make a space where it may leap and stumble in.

[rewrite]

04:58:50

Mole Wetherell – We spend about a year making a piece. We play with ideas for a number of weeks, break and then rehearse further. It is only through this process that we find out what the piece is about. *Parasite* arose out of two sources; a residency in which we had to work in a tightly confined space; and a flat in Highgate, I was living in, which was infested with cockroaches. Naturally they affected my behaviour in the flat and I became obsessed with the things. We tend to work with materials first, in *Parasite* it was the physical material of the space.

It is a blank space on which the audience projects other fictional spaces?
– I guess. We constructed a room and worked from its layout and identity which we kept quite open. We didn't want to specify a particular place in a particular time. Then we attempted to discover what would happen in that space simply by being in it. What happened were incredibly violent acts. Our relationships as a company, and as people, are quite intense. At the time socially, we were always getting pissed and fighting each other. This seeped into the rehearsals as we would work in the space for long periods without allowing ourselves to leave. We would have a few ideas, but generally we would end up getting quite

violent. I think it was partly a response to the confinement of the space. Much of the work is based on the individual personalities and presences of the performers, to an extent the structure of the work arises from this.

[mistake]

In *Parasite* the audience is enclosed in a room sitting along its four walls. They repeatedly witness an event, a violent murder. The perspective on the action changes each time the murder is re-enacted. There are lots of gaps in the scenario which are filled by the audience. For instance you will initially just hear a scene, which then reoccurs later with some of its action restored. The event is only about three minutes long but it is stretched, mutated and repeated. No one audience member sees the same piece.

02:51:08

Tim Etchells – In the early 80s we drew on visual theatre aesthetics; companies like Impact Theatre and Hesitate and Demonstrate who constructed huge illusionistic sets. Though we started out making work in that mode, it seems that our illusionistic drive has fallen away. Our sets get more and more impoverished, scrappy and brutal. In the last three shows we try to cling to some functioning centre, little rooms where we at least bring into being some desultory fiction, but, in comparison to much contemporary theatre work, we have an ambivalence towards illusionistic apparatus and a strong interest in process.

01:17:46

Joe Lawlor – For *Hope* we were influenced by many sources, particularly the photography of Joel-Peter Witkin and the processes architects go through; the aesthetics of maquettes, diagrams, models, tracings, things suggestive of incompleteness.

In Hope, *you pinned a notice on to the scenery which read 'The Set To Date'.*
– Yes, in *Hope* the presence of diagrams, floor markings, labels, and cue cards is strategic. By holding off completion a work can be changed – closure or resolution is deferred.

Is the performance a tracing too?
– As performers we are more like ciphers than characters; we perform in a neutral mode and simply say and do the things that have to be said and done. We are working with a transparent performance presence, it is certainly not psychologically full.

[missing thoughts]

Tim Etchells – For three or four years we have been interested in spaces which allude to full fictional space without ever becoming

desperate optimists are Joe Lawlor and Christine Molloy. Their work is rooted in the interrogation of narrative in performance practice. Currently they are making a piece called Dedicated *in residency at the Showroom Gallery, London.* ABOVE AND BELOW: Hope *(photos Gill Godard)*

it. Within these contexts we may occasionally put the perform-ance into fourth gear and appear to achieve a movie in the ruins of the material. So much of our process is governed by space. In rehearsals we construct a series of shambolic settings – spaces that change as the work develops. A show appears six or seven shanty towns down the road. The spatial arrangement is funda-mental to determining what and how action will take place. Few people in the mainstream work in this way.

In our previous piece *Club of No Regrets* we made a crude room in which most of the action is seen. In a coffee break Richard got up and plugged in a power saw and sawed out a window. We now talk about this moment as being part vandalism, part set building and part writing the show.

05:01:14

Matt Adams – *Stampede* is a promenade piece with six perform-ers. We have worked on the piece for nine months. Though our work is often theme-based, in *Stampede* we have much less an idea of a firm subject ground. The piece blends original text with movement. We use video to capture, frame and transmit the action onto screens. We have been collaborating with three specialists in interactive multimedia who have devised a system of pressure pads on the floor which the audience and performers use to trigger sound and video samples.

[used elsewhere]

Ju Row Farr – We are attracted to mediation because it is a major part of the way we live. It provides another layer to our performances: you see something in the flesh and simultane-ously projected on a screen. We are interested in the ways in which media change and present things. Not necessarily just film or video, but also the changes made by audio amplification.

But in theatrical space, which is a composed space (crossing light, sound, action), film and video are stubbornly discrete and pre-structured objects. Do you want a replete or coherent aesthetic?
– Projected images are strangely inanimate when you work with them. In theatrical space you often have to make media images larger and this takes them out of a domestic scale. But we are excited by this, as we are interested in the aesthetics of the club and gig scene. Because we perform in different spaces, the visual structure of a piece is often totally reorganised in relation-ship to the space we find ourselves performing in. As makers you constantly have to reassess what you planned or made previ-ously. It is more cut up but it is also more responsive.

04:49:37

Ju Row Farr – In *Stampede* the question of a coherent fictional world has become problematic for us for the first time. Moments of physical action are created and come back-to-back with each other, but the flow is strained. It seems like a fictional world is only sustained for the period of each activity and then it is cut dead. There is something within me that wants to make the performance as real as possible, because of the fact of being so close to the audience. It sounds like I need some acting lessons, but I don't want to fake sweat and I don't want to fake an activity.

[forgotten]

Why can't you let the fictions run?
Matt Adams – What we do admire about theatre is the incredible economy with which you can convey, or have an audience accept certain things, within a dramatic scenario. That ability in theatre to simply put a colander on your head and say you are a king and it becomes an accepted convention. We want the option to exploit that law. It's a three minute culture cliché, but we are supposed to be the generation who can handle watching Bugs Bunny and the next minute the Lockerbie Disaster and not find it a threatening cut. That kind of leap is a normal part of our lives. We are trying to operate on as many levels as possible, to create those kinds of juxtapositions between materials.

Ju Row Farr – We are keener to use task based activity which generates effects. But there are elements starting to come through where we've realised that if something works for an audience then it is worth doing.

Matt Adams – It would be a conveniently coherent philosophical point to say that we would never fake something on stage, but we are beginning to see that idea as something of a cul-de-sac.

02:21:21

Do you see the movements you make as plain action?
Mole Wetherell – The physical aspects of the work are based on real actions that we see everyday. We take that movement and abstract it slightly. The result is subtle, minute and gestural, though not particularly representational. I find physical theatre too clean. We are trying to get a real edge to movement.

When experiencing Parasite *there is a palpable sense of risk, not only from the performers, but from the space. Is the aim to enhance the audience's interaction, to shake our passivity?*
– We wanted to house the audience within the space, and we wanted them to see all the detail. You are forced to watch other audience members witnessing what you cannot see. You have to look very closely. There is a delicate balance because the performance is so close there's a danger of having physical audience participation, which we are not interested in. But we want the piece to have a social quality, something like being in a pub when a fight breaks out and you can't get away. The next piece *To Speak and Not be Heard* will have a similar quality. The

Reckless Sleepers aim to explore visual ideas through a strong physical language in a theatrical context. The company was formed in 1989 by artistic director Mole Wetherell and artist Dan Rogers. ABOVE: Parasite *(photo Hugo Glendinning)*

performers will probably all be talking at the same time, so you are in a room hearing fragments of different conversations, tiny parts of stories, personal material and statements.

05:19:59

What motivated you to produce performance rather than becoming involved with political action?

Matt Adams – One of our driving aspirations was to make work that accentuated and was entirely dependent upon its 'liveness', work that could not happen in any other environment or in any other way, and could not be reproduced in any other medium. A political agenda is extremely important for us on personal and artistic levels. We are wary of oblique political attitudes in work. The issues of accessibility, what kind of audience we reach, and in what context, are essential to us and recurrent questions for the work itself. When we are making we are always asking ourselves 'is it clear?', 'does it read?', 'who does it read to?'

We play to diverse audiences in contexts as distinct as Council run youth venues and established gallery spaces. We started out with a strong sense of a political agenda about speaking to an audience on issues. We are still wrestling with that naive, fresh, optimistic idea that you could do such a thing.

[clear?]

06:14:47

Though it appears accessible, work which announces itself as issue or theme based often establishes hierarchies of meaning. Is it restrictive to work under single themes, and do the audience's possible readings get subsumed by those big unitary signs?
– We are aware of that, but we see it as a liberating restriction. It gives us confidence to know that we are working on solid ground. We began making performance work with a feeling that Post-Modernism had run its course, and that whilst it was valid to talk about media culture, hyper-reality and unstable meanings, there was still a very concrete and meaningful world in which people do suffer and do get shot. The Gulf War did happen, and there are still political issues about power and who holds it and what they do with it.

[nothing said]

02:46:39

Mole Wetherell – We don't work within a political framework. I'm not sure how that could be our role. We want to produce work with many possible readings. It seems that to have strongly political work this idea would have to be lost.

06:15:03

Matt Adams – Obviously Forced Entertainment are right – you cannot control what people do with the work. We just have a different attitude to political action. Within the fabric of our work there are explicit references to the fact that people are acting politically all the time. Though we both appropriate texts and images from real life, we bring a documentary quality to our work. We are keen not to create a replete fictional world. We use recordings of actual events taking place, intrusions and footnotes from an immediately recognisable real world. In *Stampede* we show a three minute film of the guy standing in front of a tank in Tiananmen Square. The audience is made to stand in front of this image. No explicit reference is made to this event by any of the performers. As audience members you are faced with a question, an assault on the work as solely a piece of art.

[repetition]

There is a bottom line at which politics is about making a simplification and going with that. I'm not saying that I want our audiences to come out of pieces and make instant public actions, but I do want them to have had a collective political experience in an environment where they felt something in relation to other people. Putting a live audience in a place and getting ideas going has the potential to generate conflagrations. We still hold that ridiculous and foolish aspiration that you may change people's lives.

03:18:29

There has been much loose talk recently about relativism and nihilism, it seems the British Live Art scene is gripped by a rediscovery of value. I'm interested in the ways in which your work understands and represents the dilemma of belief. Hope has a kind of pragmatism, it is concerned with saying in detail what can be believed in. Whereas, I think Forced Entertainment's work is more hesitant, less particular and concerned with the contingency of belief.

[repetition]

Joe Lawlor – Ethical and moral values are never too faraway from our work. In *Hope* we used a text which was a list of beliefs. The lack of opacity and lyricism in our texts made them way too crude for some people. We wanted, without any irony, to just say the things we believed in, perhaps because ethically they needed to be said. For some people it sounded glib and simplistic, but I think that says as much about the receiver as it does about the person making the statements. Although Forced Entertainment and ourselves share an ethical and spiritual ground, our work is less interested in lyricism, romance, the parody of values and more interested in the action of statement.

65

Formed in 1991, Blast Theory make promenade performances that use elements of theatre, dance, video and computers. The group collaborates with people from a wide range of disciplines, from DJs to installation artists. Matt Adams and Ju Row Farr are members of the co-operative.
ABOVE: Stampede *(photo Anne Brassier)*

WOMEN'S VOICES
NICOLA OXLEY

The demise of Modernism, located some 25 years ago, was instrumental in the rupture with traditional monolithic views of culture, and has led many women artists to reappraise their positions and strategies. The feminisation of theory, along with women's exploration of disciplines usually found outside the territory of art, has shed new light on the notion of sexual difference. Psychoanalysis, often described as a masculine discourse to subjugate women, has been turned into a strategy to assess and critique traditional male/female relationships. Artists and writers are historically constructed as individuals who subsist on their singularity, an assumption which continues into the present-day. I felt it would be important to continue instigating new relationships with other practitioners, both in, as well as outside of the realm of art production. The following text is the outcome of a collaboration with psychotherapist Wil Pennycook-Greaves and focuses on an ongoing dialogue with women in the United Kingdom.

There is no doubt that the process of finding a voice, of expressing desire and of creating images which belong to women has been a long one, and one which is still precarious, for traditional belief structures continue to exert their influence. The loss that concerns us here, is the access to the apprehending self. Power struggles should not involve a loss, or giving up, of ways of feeling and relating which are important in the making of work.

Isolation should not be the price to pay for independence. However, it seems that there is great fear and anxiety about managing difference, and the pressure of assimilation is as great as it ever was. Many women are choosing to go through an art training that demands understanding and analysis of their own practice in relation to the art market, together with the necessity of a theoretical position *vis-à-vis* their work. Theory has become a sexy art form. Self-reflection and the ability to experience feelings and translate them is a fundamental part of the process of making work. Theory and knowledge are important in the understanding of that process. Theory should grow out of practice and not the other way around. Has art appropriated theory, and attached it without integrating it and without taking responsibility for increasing understanding? What therefore appears to empower women, that is, the taking hold of theory, may in subtle ways, inhibit the difficult processes of production. It is not being said here that theory is a negative influence but that it should be seen in context. Defining and explaining is in danger of replacing exploring, leading to a potential loss of the image. Power, it seems to us, is in the capacity to connect not in the capacity to detach. Is the paradox that theory emasculates art? Are women hijacking theory? Is the belief that it is where power lies a false one? And is the appropriation of it detracting from the content of their work?

There are many dilemmas in the making of work. One is whether making work is a private or public activity: who is one speaking to, wanting to touch, affect. Is the way that you view the world important? We live in a multicultural world where diversity is a necessity and yet the creation of ghettos is rife. We talk only to those that we know, or to the media. Are artists becoming media people, speaking to everyone and no one? The desire to be seen may be replacing the desire to create, leading to the phenomenon of the artist as personality. The personal is no longer the political, it is the artificial. The rush now is not to get into the art studio but to get into the television studio. What appears as talking to each other, misses the point that in order to create a dialogue, you need to be able to consider another point of view. We now have soliloquies rather than conversations.

The media and telecommunications are here to stay. With ever more accessible and available hardware, we can communicate with each other around the world. Yet, do we know what it is that we want to say? Do we have a point of view? We have become used to the narcissistic viewpoint where there is no other, that assumes that everyone is the same as the subject. How do we generate questions about the nature of making work? It seems that increasingly disciplines are being plundered without the acknowledgement that there are boundaries and without the understanding that these boundaries are fundamental to the existence of each activity. There seems to be an anxiety about knowing everything. The creative endeavour may, however, involve a different activity, that of 'not knowing', described by the poet John Keats as 'a capacity to be in doubts and uncertainties without any irritable searching after fact and reason'. This opens up a whole area of debate and potential dialogue between artists and others. Artists have different ways of exploring the same wishes, and there is richness in experiencing the difference and similarities. Perhaps now, more than ever, we need to be able to move on from the fear that, different points of view, and the potential conflicts, undermine the position of strength offered by a multiplicity of voices. Dialectically there is nothing to lose.

Nicola Oxley is a Senior Lecturer in Fine Art at London's Guildhall University, co-author of Installation Art, *Thames & Hudson 1994, co-director of the Museum of Installation and a practising artist.*

Mary Kelly Andrea Fisher Avis Newman Cathy de Monchaux Kate Smith Sharon Kivland Ann Bean Amanda Faulkner Nicky Hirst Susan Trangmar Lisa Milroy Ann Talentine Angela Bulloch Shelagh Wakely Anya Gallaccio Rose Finn Kelcey Cornelia Parker Gillian Wearing Sam Taylor Wood Hannah Collins Monica Ross Mona Hatoum Helen Chadwick Bobby Baker Shirazeh Houshiary Lucia Nogueira Kathy Prendergast Susan Hiller Paula Rego Louise Tonkin Rachel Whiteread Phyllis Mahon Anne Seagrave Zarina Bhimji Virginia Nimarkoh Sonia Boyce Debbie Duffin Gloria Carlos Fiona Rae Sarah Lucas Judith Cowan Yoko Terauchi Reiko Kubo Dorothy Cross Alanna O'Kelly Rita Duffy Cecily Brennan Aileen Mackeogh Karen Henderson Fiona Banner Lucy Gunning Deborah Henley Maggie Hambling Maggie Ellenby Tina Keane Melanie Counsell Hermione Wiltshire Abigail Lane Eileen Cooper Glenys Johnson Katherine Clarke Sue Morris Amy Eshoo Silvia Ziranek Rosie Leventon Jo Stockham Christine Borland Clare Charnley Louise Wilson Jane Wilson Alison Wilding Sara Charlesworth Rose English Claire Joy Therese Oulton Mariko Mori Rachel Evans Jane Mulfinger Siobhan Wall Rose Garrard Sue Arrowsmith Catherine Yass Mary Jane Opie Nicola Hicks Helen Thompson Ursula McCannell Verdi Yahooda Kate Whiteford Rita Keegan Permindar Kaur Valerie Brown Leslie Sanderson Glenys Barton Carole Hodgson Jane Joseph Laura Ford Imogen Stidworthy Gabrielle Venus Bridget Riley Edwina Leapman Rita Donagh Gillian Ayres Rosemary Butcher Alexis Hunter Caroline Russell Jessica Matlock Linda Sgoluppi Kate Blacker Marty St James Ann Wilson Deborah Thomas Clare Carswell Lisa Watt Melanie Poole Fiona Wright Suzanne Treister Louise Blair Caroline Broadhead Sarah Brooker Fran Cottell Sokari Douglas Camp Susie Freeman Suzanne Heron Cas Holmes Bridget Bailey Yolande Snaith Deb Thomas Jenny Wiggins Lois Williams Shelagh Cluett Maria Chevska Tanya Kovat Fran Hegarty Vicky Hawkins Eileen Agar Sutapa Biswas Gwen Fereday Gwen Hardie Bethan Huws Lubaina Himid Loraine Leeson aiv Vicken Parsons Julia Wood Hannah Vowles Nicky Bell Valerie Walkerdine Sophie Ryder Jacqueline Moreau Rosa Lee Prullella Clough Annie Griffin Wendy Taylor Catherine Roche Maxine Mason Chantal Joffe Suzanne Ajamian Claire Barclay Margaret Neve Ana Maria Pacheco Madeleine Stringberg Laetitia Yhap Julia Ball Vivien Blackett Sandra Blow Elizabeth Blackadder Anne Bruce Felicity Charlton Ann Dowker Mary Fedden Rebecca Fortnum Vit Hopley Maud Sulter Mary Husted Tess Jaray Ghisha Koenig Deanna Petherbridge Celia Paul Paula Sanders Mandy Havers Susan Tebby Tam Giles Fay Goodwin Melanie Manchot Suky Best Jane Bawn Nancy Honey Lana Wong Sue Andrews Mari Mahr Rosie Martin Grace Robertson Elizabeth Williams Della Grace Jenny Mathews Janine Weidal Ingrid Pollard Joy Gregory Dorothy Bohm Anna Fox Christina McBride Sirka Liisa Konttinen Jean Baird Lindell Reilly Monica Chau Christina Berry Natalie Turned

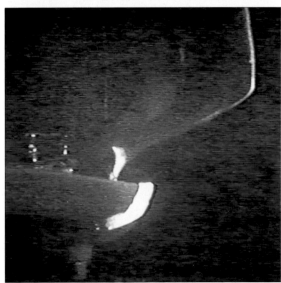

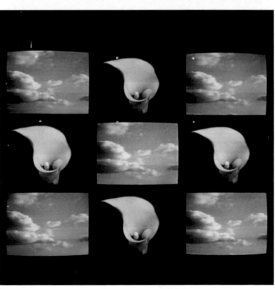

PAGE 70: Phyllida Barlow, Object for Furniture, 1994; OPPOSITE: Katherine Meynell, Eat, 1992, Kettles Yard, Cambridge; FROM ABOVE: Amanda Wilson, Through Attitude, Exclusion and Faithfulness, 1991, installation detail; Anne Eggebert, The Visit of a Stranger, 1994, installation detail, Queens Tower, Imperial College; Amanda Wilson, Through Attitude, Exclusion and Faithfulness, 1991, performance video; Katherine Meynell, Moonrise, 1989, video wall, Tate Gallery, Liverpool

The women artists selected for these pages are not meant to illustrate the text. Rather, their work is indicative of the wide concerns of a critical practice. Their work is not built upon a protective insularity, but instead asserts its presence within an increasingly fragmented, yet institutionalised experience. The scope of their work does not suggest its interchangeability or indifference, but focuses our attention on 'the realisation that our culture is neither as homogeneous or as monolithic as we once believed it to be.'

OPPOSITE: Marion Kalmus, Well, 1994; FROM ABOVE, L TO R: Rose Frain, Towards an Archaeology of the Unconscious, Cabinet 1, (Press), steel, iron, china, ink, mouse-tail, silver, vellum, saltwater, earth, blood, honey, lead, photo-image, wood, brass; Nicola Oxley, Untitled, 1994, Museum of Installation, Site 8, Peterborough Museum; Rosemarie McGoldrick, Bone: cast, painted and arranged; Caroline Wilkinson, Fugitive, 1993, Museum of Installation

Ross Sinclair, United States, Diary . . . Los Angeles 12 April 1992, *from Transmission Gallery, Glasgow/City Racing, London exchange show*

WHEN ARE YOU LEAVING?
LIAM GILLICK

There comes a time when groups of artists begin to concentrate upon the point at which they emerged. The process is somewhat inevitable and varies in depth depending on the people involved. This inevitability is due to repositioning and the increasing desire to differentiate varied practices. It is arguable that at the beginning a set of people show potential rather than precise objectives. Therefore, it is often difficult to tell the difference between one promising artist and another. The examination of a starting point is aided by media attention. Right from the start the process of assessment is withdrawn from the artist's complete control, and a story develops in parallel to the events as they are perceived by the artists themselves. Mistakes are amplified and half-truths are exploited by both sides. These distortions are often in the interest of only some of the artists involved. So people start to look back. Generally this is done in order to rationalise the perceived significance of the artist's break with whatever happened to be going on just before their emergence. Whether or not the more recent work was ever made with the intention of destabilising what had come before is irrelevant. The desire to reassess is not based on a desire for accuracy it is to do with aiding the continuation of a set of arguments and justifications.

With recent British art, this process of re-examination is inextricably linked with the way the work has been contextualised here. It is interesting therefore to address the way recent British art has been discussed in phenomenological terms. It is tempting to stick to precisely remembered details. To talk about how it was German dealers who first dragged reluctant English galleries to the Docklands in the late 80s – or how some artists were surprised at the curator credits that got tacked onto catalogues at the same time. But who cares? He who pays the printer sets the colophon. And anyway, would it be interesting if people believed that Gary Hume curated 'Modern Medicine' or that Rachel Whiteread went to Goldsmiths'? The point is that a strange mix of self-determination and generalised commentary has provided a peculiar situation here, one that affects the way that work is made and the way in which it is read.

What seems to have been overlooked is the way in which a group of artists who have consistently been lumped together were not a group at all. What characterises the work is activity. Artists constantly operating and repositioning within a peculiar intellectual vacuum that led to the most perverse form of competition to have emerged during the Thatcher years. This has been combined with a desire to escape, in order to find a validating context. This has usually meant showing in other countries. And it is often dealers, curators and critics from the rest of Europe and America who have taken the greatest initial risk with recent art. Now this seems to contradict most of the writing about young artists from Britain in the past few years. In this country it always seems necessary to focus blame upon a particular academy rather than upon ideas. It must have something to do with the effects of a public school system.

This vague attempt to pin things down is not without its benefits. It certainly permits multiple activity beneath an all encompassing umbrella, and provides a way to avoid specific contradictions. Telling you everything and nothing about an individual or group. An aura can then be created that essentially glows with tolerance. A state of affairs that is not based upon the analysis of specific concepts but upon the accidental proximity of artists or people. Of course the various characters involved talk to each other, and sometimes have the benefit of seeing each other's work at the primary stage of production, but this is not necessarily the key to understanding what has taken place. This is not to remove all the credit from the education system, rather it is important to ensure that it doesn't get all the blame. The significant thing about art from this country in the last few years has been the artist's desire to peel away and engage with other systems and other debates.

Yet people still come here in search of the source of that escape. They probably meet the artists heading in the opposite direction at the airport. And like a British film from the early 60s, set in a Northern industrial town, they seem to only find a peculiar combination of authenticity, absence, arrogance and promise. It is important to recognise the way that all of this leads to flexibility. That it leads to the production of things, because people are not argued into inactivity. And it might be suggested that the only way to deal with such potential is to look at the conditions that fostered it. There is a necessity to examine the general state of receptiveness in this country, and the concurrent desire to leave and engage with some else's debate.

It has become normal to overhear the following truncated conversation: 'What are you working on at the moment?' 'Oh I've just got back from Berlin/Paris/New York/Azerbaijan.' This is fine. It indicates a degree of movement and engagement that is often undervalued. Shorthand for 'I am making art.' The moment that this engagement became real, the whole idea of 'group', fragile as it already was, collapsed into itself, and has never really recovered. This is connected to a clash of ideologies. People, from this country, going elsewhere and finding a set of ethically

Mud slinger no.1

OPPOSITE: Angela Bulloch, Mudslinger No 1, *1993, CCC Tours, France (photo François Poivret), FROM ABOVE, LEFT TO RIGHT: Gillian Wearing, photographs from 'Signs that say what you want them to say . . .', 1992-3; Gary Hume,* Naturalist, *1992, panel one – oil on paper, panels two and three – collage on canvas, 243.8 x 355.6cm; Damien Hirst,* Still Pursuing Impossible Desires, *1992, steel, glass, rubber, household gloss paint, canvas, pupae and butterflies*

'New Art from Scotland', 1994, CCA, Glasgow; ABOVE:
Part III; CENTRE: Part II; BELOW: Henry Bond, The
Romance of Soap Making, 1995, videostill

based loyalties, and factions that were prepared to welcome some producers in order to back up ongoing discussions. The British artists were the producers and the people maintaining flickering ideologies in the rest of the Western art world were the receptors. The barren individualist vacuum foisted upon this country, allowed the development of a set of reasonably self-interested artists, and beyond their self-organised shows here was a ready and waiting international debate about the role of the artist. Such a discussion, when framed within the terms of recent Post-Modernism, was inevitably capable of absorbing all the contradictions that British artists were prepared to throw at it.

One of the great claims in Britain has been that we exist within a primarily literary tradition, whilst just off to the side is a great theatrical tradition. Both are held up as examples of successful populist art forms. Yet suppose, for a minute, that there is in fact no real literary tradition and that theatre is nothing more than embarrassing television. Either way, we have a society that, when under pressure, pleads artistic engagement via books and performance rather than visual art – which includes design, film, television and music. In the meantime, other societies proceed to analyse the really powerful art forms; abstraction, deconstruction, media and communication. However, the literary culture sticks to its guns. There is no need to worry about social anthropology or the way society reframes itself. We have books to write. Not books about what goes on, but just books. What would happen if that society realised that its literary tradition, while real enough, seeing as it is imagined to be real, was no more, or less, significant than the literary tradition in other places. Not only that, but other places had used writing in order to come to terms with the apparent contradictions of our present situation.

On the other hand, few social commentators anywhere would deny the peculiarity of dynamic British subculture. A subculture that quickly became the mainstream. It is well known that most of the key players in this original group of musicians and designers in the 60s, went to art schools or specialised in art at technical colleges. And now of course they would often like to become re-engaged with the mainstream art world. So David Bowie wants to meet young, New York based, British artist and dealer Gavin Brown, even though he is associated with *Modern Painters* magazine. Weirder chameleon behaviour than in his heyday. So now we have a non-group of artists, who talk to each other in terms which sound like a airport departure board and a group of musicians who would like to engage with this non-scene. What artists have learnt from more sophisticated forms of popular culture is that the creation of an aura of activity can be everything.

This reversal creates interesting art. It is at the root of our destabilised situation. It mirrors the contradictions inherent in the rest of society. As such art in Britain is valid in a way that it was rarely valid in the past. You have a dynamic visual culture, capable of rapid moves in different directions, and it is now complemented by a complex contemporary art world that has realised the mythology of the narrative tradition, and replaced it

with 'text'. The story has become a visual Haiku. There is a great deal of stealing and appropriation going on. And there are people leaving and coming back. So when did all this begin and what were the key points in this desire to get out?

Most of the major galleries involved in the recent rise of British art have not been British; Karsten Schubert is German, Maureen Paley is American and Laure Genillard is Swiss. OK, Jay Jopling looks and sounds British but he's probably not really from this country. Anyway, he is a late addition. At the beginning, the German and American dealers who were interested in what was going on, went and told the English dealers who were all German and American too. These people inevitably provided a way out of Britain right from the start. This was provided without having to leave the country. Just by going to Karsten Schubert gallery you could enter the suburbs of Berlin, and Interim Art was always a little bit New York. These galleries were significant for their initial concentration on an international scene. Nicholas Logsdail, from the Lisson Gallery, also began, 15 or so years earlier, by showing artists from outside Britain. This *mélange* created a certain ease, allowing new artists to move immediately into a more internationalist dialogue, but this is where the good and the bad begins.

English formalist bullshit, all look and no content. The visual equivalent of a discarded Monty Python sketch. The problem with bothering to produce things within this peculiar environment, is that there is a powerful misreading of Post-Modernism at work. Most Post-Modern theory, of any substance, was intended to analyse society in order to realign the Marxist trajectory. Only here could you overhear someone ask a Frenchman the politics of a central figure of recent French theory, and find the answer was that of course he was a Marxist. The questioner was mildly stunned and tried to realign the original enquiry; surely Post-Modernism has something to do with individuality? It justified bad buildings and amoralism. We are all, myself included, victims of the rereadings of other people's analysis, but everyone resolutely continues to produce. Regardless of the complications, or the layers of irony, that can form a dense blanket over the art being made elsewhere. The British art world is not art school led, even if that would appear to provide an easy rationalisation of recent activity. The situation here is flexible in the extreme, and permits entry to the semi-debate at all levels. The development of context is always an issue that disturbs the leading participants who are involved in making and trying to exhibit work. It is inappropriate to mention specific artists, as we can all play the game of the development of the non-group. It is rather more interesting to feel the aura and accept the fact that the most interesting work has developed from the possession of a plane ticket and a desire to engage in someone else's debate.

Since leaving Goldsmith's College in 1987, Liam Gillick has exhibited in a number of galleries, both in Britain and abroad, he has been involved with a number of book projects, including Technique Anglais, *Thames and Hudson, 1988, and is a partner in the publishing company G-W Press.*

PARALLEL CONJUNCTION
MARIO FLECHA

Parallel Line One

Parallel lines, according to *The Concise Oxford English Dictionary*, are two lines continuously equidistant. This reflects the state of art in the United Kingdom today. One line, produced by artists from racial minorities, is highly political and on the fringe. The other line emanates from the white man, based on European concepts and tradition, and provides a more official account of events.

To be able to comprehend this situation, where two sets of mainstream ideas are parallel, it is necessary to remember that we are close to the end of this century and that visual art has been through one of one the most dynamic periods of its history. The UK, with its private and public galleries, is living through one of those strange times in history where the work of many people reaches fruition. Artists, colleges and institutions who support visual art have been working together in a coherent way, creating the sense of excitement that the UK art world enjoys.

The post-imperialist artists are confronted with a new set of realities; a multiracial society, the collapse of the welfare state, unemployment, postfeminism, sexuality, gender, the Aids epidemic and poverty. Perhaps in this new situation a conjunction of these two conflicting worlds is possible. To contextualise all these elements, presented as a jigsaw, it is necessary to refer to the past and reconcile it with the present.

The colonial past is reflected in today's multiracial society as a result of the emigration of people from the colonies towards the centre of the old empire. Since the end of the Second World War the disintegration of the empire has accelerated the influx of people from other races to live in the British Isles. After an initial silence and victimisation, the second and third generation of immigrants are developing a complex and interesting language, articulating their own voice, addressing issues concerning their cultural identity, eroding the prejudice to which they were subjected and beginning to assert their rights. Since there is no other European country with such a heterogeneous population it is no surprise that it is where these politicised minority artists emerge, articulating a broad way of expressing themselves, integrating new and old disciplines in their art; including painting, sculpture, video, mixed-media, performance, photo installation et cetera.

They are part of the unofficial history. Rasheed Araeen who was exhibiting at the South London Gallery in 1994, is a Pakistani artist, curator, critic and writer who has lived in London for the last 30 years. As a founder member of Black Art, a group formed by immigrant artists against racism in Britain, developing his political and cultural interest through his art practice has been one of critical interest. The most controversial work he has produced was an installation at the Showroom Gallery, London in 1988. Named *A Long Walk in the Wilderness* it was a direct appropriation of a Richard Long piece which incensed the art establishment. In his new work he uses a grid format of nine panels, where each corner panel has been painted green forming a cross in the middle, which he uses with narrative images. His work is a dry intellectual exercise reminding us that the debate between coloniser and colonised is not over.

White Stallion, one of the series of four works on the green panels, symbolises not only the Islamic tradition but argues that minimalist artists like Donald Judd or Ad Reinhardt have taken their ideas from the Islamic culture and promoted it as if it were their own. In one of the arms of the cross, four surveillance planes come into land. Meanwhile, the central image is of Saddam Hussein on a rampant white horse holding a flag with the inscription 'Allah is great'. Saddam Hussein's image is from a popular poster, depicting him as a hero who challenged the western allies in the Gulf War. As a background he has taken an image from a television screen of a USA press conference room in which are hanging the American and Saudi Arabian flags.

Describing the work in the exhibition catalogue Paul Overy stated that:

> The work clearly does not celebrate, nor does it glorify either 'side', but rather problematises the complex dynamics of war and its representation through different media by drawing attention to the essentially racist origins of the war and the way in which it is represented through images and language.

Oh Dear, Oh Dear What a Mess You Have Made!, is at first glance an appropriation of the work of Jackson Pollock but if we look more carefully we can see, hidden between splashes of colour, that he has paint barbed wire. It is a curious painting, used to mark limits and provide barriers. Barbed wire is usually clearly visible but Rasheed reminds us that even when you don't see them the limits imposed by the oppressor are there.

A new generation of artists of multiracial origins participated in an exhibition commemorating 500 years since the discovery of America by Columbus. Galleries in three ports; the Blue Coat Gallery in Liverpool, the Arnofini Gallery in Bristol and Hull Time Based Art organised an exhibition called 'Trophies of Empire'. The starting points for the project were provided by an information pack by Keith Piper, Abdullah Badwi and researcher Janice

PAGE 82: Rebecca Scott,
Brothers and Sisters, *1994,
installation Mario Flecha Gallery;
ABOVE: Mark Wallinger,* Foun-
tain, *1992, installation Anthony
Reynolds Gallery, London;
BELOW: Lucia Nogueira,* Ends
without End, *1992, detail*

Cheddie. The 15 artists' response was that there was little to celebrate over 500 years of commerce and slavery.

The participating artists included Paul Clarkson, a painter born in Liverpool, whose narrative painting challenges the official history, and Carole Drake, born in Bristol, whose installation *Commemoration Day* seeks to expose the denial of Colston's trading in the life of African people. Nina Edge's mixed-media installation are three small objects standing on photographic tripods with names like *Multicultural peepshow*. Edwina Fitzpatrick's *Terra* mixed-media installation is a didactic piece showing the history of the exploitation of our planet and more specifically that of coffee, taken from around the world to satisfy the needs of the Europeans. Sunil Gupta, born in India presents eight mural images depicting fascism, sexuality and the consumer society in photographic representations. Bandele Iyapo is a performer from Trinidad. He worked with the Bristol community mixing people of different race, sex and age in an attempt to create an awareness of black people in St Pauls and Easton in a white middle-class audience at the Arnolfini Gallery. Rita Keegan, Juginer Iamba, Shaheen Merali, Keith Piper, Donald Rodney, Veena Stephenson were the other participants.

The curatorial work of this issue-based exhibition, where sensitive subjects such as race and slavery were addressed, was exceptional. The difficulty for an exhibition of this kind lies in seeing the divide between them/aggressor and us/victim as irreconcilable opposites.

Parallel Line Two
Well into the Thatcher era, close to the end of the 80s, a more aggressive style of artist began to appear, and Goldsmith's College graduates set the trend: highly professional and ambitious, Damian Hirst is perhaps the most notable. Here they nurture a very distinctive brand of artist: Mark Wallinger, Cathy de Monchaux, Rebecca Scott, Simon Linke, Clare Joy, Glenn Brown, Jordan Baseman, Perry Roberts, Caroline Russell, Catherine Yass, Graham Gussin, Matthew Collishaw, Pat Kaufman, Anya Gallacio, Stephen Hepworth, Fiona Rae and Hamad Butt to name but a few.

Rebecca Scott's paintings and knitting have the intention of undermining the myth of male superiority. In the early paintings she took images from the photographs in pornography magazines and cards, produced mainly for consumption by the gay community. The paintings are skilfully drawn using rich, lush colours and depict naked boys. In *Red Porsche* the boy is holding his erect penis with both hands, an empty, perplexed look on his face. A female painter exposes men in the same way that man has been exposing woman for centuries, the man becomes an object, and for the male audience, reacting immediately and taking the moral high ground, this is pornography.

Then came the flower paintings in conjunction with car engines, equating as a starting point female-flowers, male-car engines. Using this concept she displays all her skill as a painter, the colours exploding on the canvas, using layer after layer, building up a tactile texture. Some of the large paintings combine flowers and car engines in an attempt to reconcile the sexes. In another, a linear drawing of genitalia is hidden by what appears to be an innocent painting of flowers.

Lately, in the installation *Brothers and Sister*, she uses nine knitted balls strewn across the floor of the gallery, each of approximately one metre in diameter, in strong coloured segments like a beach ball. At first glance it is very difficult to see what is on them, but on closer inspection it is possible to see the depiction of a flaccid penis in each segment. Through the softness of the medium they lose any notion of a threatening phallic presence.

Rebecca Scott's preoccupation with the role of women and how they are portrayed by a patriarchal society continues and she challenges its assumptions and distorts them, producing a new and uncomfortable dimension. The simplicity of the images kills the menacing power as in *Freudian Posy* in which the enormous flowers, behind a grid, hide the silhouette of a pair of scissors.

Her last installation, *Brothers and Sisters* was a more relaxed statement. Using the colourful balls strewn on the floor, with their images of flaccid penises, looking like a rainbow she appeared to be saying 'the fight is not over but now I can play'.

Mark Wallinger, the epitome of English eccentricity, is an accomplished painter as well as installation artist. At Anthony Reynolds Gallery a red hose pipe went through the glass of the front window, pumping water constantly onto the street. Recently, following his passion for racehorses he bought a horse which he called *A Real Work of Art*.

Pat Kaufman, an American artist based in London, works in the minimalist tradition. In her wall-pieces like *Dual,* where two house shapes are united, one side ebony, the other steel, the resonance of the absence of narrative and expression is captured.

Jordan Baseman's last installation *f is for love* covers a wall with human hair. A naked letter f on the right side, is related directly to William Blake's *Songs of Innocence* and *Songs of Experience*. F is for fear – to fall in love at the end of this century implies a loss of innocence with dangerous consequences.

Many other artists unrelated to Goldsmith's College, Rose Finn Kelcey, Dean Whatmuff, Amikam Torem, Nikki Bell, Ben Langlands, Gerard Williams, David Austen, Callum Innes, Elizabeth Magill and Rachel Whiteread are producing exceptional work.

Conjunction
Is there any possibility that the parallels can reach a point of conjunction? In mathematical terms they will meet at infinity. In my analogy the lines illustrated can become united through a universal discourse thus breaking national boundaries.

Hamad Butt born in Pakistan, was one of the most promising artists, until after only two exhibitions he died of Aids, but the impact of his work transcends his materiality and the Tate Gallery will include his work in its exhibition 'Rites of Passage' in July

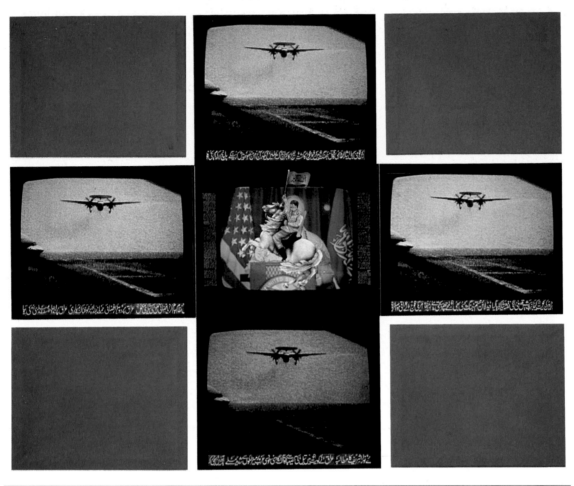

*FROM ABOVE: Rasheed Araeen,
White Stallion, 1991; Pat Kauf-man,
Dual, 1991, mild steel and
ebonised wood, 61.5 x 78 x 7.5cm*

1995, curated by Stuart Morgan. Hamad was interested in art and science and his knowledge of his own illness made him work with dangerous materials, pushing his experience to the limits as any error in their manipulation could be fatal. Using the method and discipline of an alchemist, he repeated the same actions pursuing not the transmutation of the substance but of himself.

Transmission, his first exhibition in 1990 at the Milch Gallery in London, referred to scriptural exegesis, science fiction and Aids, and involved using protective goggles to contemplate the circle of ultraviolet reading lamps and glass books. Typical of his work, he is playing with the fragility of our being as not using the safety measure of the goggles meant one could be blinded.

His second, and last, installation at the John Hansard Gallery in Southampton, *Familiars,* displayed halogens (iodine bromine and chlorine) in solid, liquid and gaseous form respectively. In this installation Hamad develops his interest in 'metachemics', his private equivalent to metaphysics. These enormous glass bubbles of poisonous chlorine gas with their potential to explode again exposed him and us to a confrontation with destruction.

His interest in alchemy as an extension of his art made him formulate the possibility of a 'metachemist'. In his statement he concludes that:

Metachemics will consider, then, the apprehensions that inform the extent of our acknowledgement of substance. The term substance hereby incorporates the classical alchemical definition with its root in the Aristotelian correspondence of essences and attributes (or accidents) with, a chemical diagnosis of each substances' curative and toxic indications and, the periodicity, or chemical kinship, of the elements involved.

It is possible to hear Lucia Nogueira's voice and movement in her work. They speak to us in a primitive code transforming daily objects into objects of art. Like a shaman she pronounces incomprehensible words to communicate and the effects they produce are beyond our rationality. At the Ikon Gallery in Birmingham she scattered casually on the floor a bunch of cables; pressing against a column the wheel of a tricycle with a piece of cable holding it. A table turned on its back *'No times for commas'*, with a brown bag inside jumping without direction or aim. In another piece a sheet of broken glass lies on the floor with a spindle on top. Her discourse is directed to our unconsciousness. There is no rational association from which to explain with words the experience of seeing.

The Institution, the Artist, the Collector

Perhaps the most bizarre debate at the moment is between those who, in a conservative way, believe art is only expressed by paintings or sculpture and those who think that art needs to be supported by an idea and that it does not matter what material is used. This is irrelevant as it is easy to understand that after centuries of painting artists have lost the necessary vitality and imagination the medium requires. One only has to consider Uccello and his obsession with perspective, the Black Painting of Malevich or the vitality of the American abstract expressionists and the others that followed. Certainly, to express an idea with a certain degree of originality and break the paralysis that painting is currently suffering requires a great effort of the imagination but this does not mean that painting is dead. However, this sense of antagonistic activities is a delusion. What is important are the concepts and the search to express them in the way that best suits the individual artist's ability to capture the imagination of the people.

Mario Flecha was born in Buenos Aires and now lives London, he was the director of the Mario Flecha Gallery from 1987-93, he is a freelance curator and the publisher of Untitled, *a British art magazine that examines contemporary art.*

Ecstasy of Fumbling (portrait of the artist in a gas alert), *1991, oil and mixed media on canvas*

JOHN KEANE
AN INTERVIEW WITH ORIANA BADDELEY

Oriana Baddeley – *We first met in 1978, and even at that point you seemed to be fascinated with the intersection of history, the political moment, and art.*

John Keane – I think I was, but without ever quite realising what it was I was interested in. I spent a good few years just trying to find the language, having very little confidence about what I was doing and getting pretty minimal feedback, which at that time was quite debilitating and depressing. But I kept working quite doggedly. And then, I suppose, my way of working began to loosen up and become more direct and, in some ways, less self-conscious. That also coincided with beginning to find a voice of my own, realising what it was that interested me, which had a lot to do with what I saw going on around me in the world. One of the main catalysts for that, I think, was the Falklands War, which just as an historical event was quite a shock to me. I'm of the post Second World War generation, and the country had never really been at war, and so for this to happen, in my late 20s, was quite a shock, and I began to process that in some ways through my work. It was a catalyst, a starting point, and historically in my development it was quite important. Most of what I'd done before that, I look back on now and I feel I was floundering around rather. Perhaps people looking back on what I did then would see a link in some ways, that there was obviously some interest, a political, topical and historical interest going on there which relates to the work I'd done so far.

There was a recognition that accessible subject matter was still interesting, at a point when maybe that wasn't fashionable.
– I agree. The legacy of art school and the contemporary art scene was a kind of orthodoxy, of what was an acceptable way to work. I think where I came into my own was realising 'to hell with all that' and just working the way I wanted to. Obviously I would take into account whatever else was going on, but I realised what was important to me and tried to bring that into my work.

But there was also an interest in popular culture when a lot of other artists in the 70s worked in far more theoretical areas.
– Yes, I found all that conceptualism and minimalism very dreary indeed, and I think it had a lot to do with antagonising not the art public, but the general public in a way. To me painting was a vehicle of communication, and if you're not communicating, you might as well forget about it.

There was a bit of aggression, I remember your constructivist

deck chair, it was a bit like sitting on the conceptualists.
– There was that, and I was taking the piss as well, there was a heavy irony, and that continues in many ways in my attitude towards art as being able to achieve anything. But irony now is something rather disdainful, because it has become such an orthodox item of post-modernist detachment, which disturbs me.

Whilst finding a visual language, your early explorations seemed to be about distance and objectivity; working more in non-subjective mediums, almost parodying print techniques.
– I think it was to do with my feelings about actually having to make a mark on a canvas, it sounds ludicrous but it's quite problematic. If you've got a subject, how do you tackle it, what do you do with it? And I did use things like airbrush in paintings, which was a way of slightly removing myself from the canvas, you could be quite gestural with it, but it's essentially flat.

Was it an ironic gestural presence, as there is a sense of you putting a mechanical process between yourself and the canvas?
– Yes, but I think where the watershed came was around the Falklands War, 1982, and it also coincided with a big movement back towards painting, or painting being re-evaluated then, and I thought, 'Well, to hell with this, just get stuck in and make marks, slap the paint around,' and I began to get involved in that and just began to enjoy the medium, and learn a lot as well. If I look back to how I actually handled paint then, there are many things, just in terms of technique and what you can do with paint, that I have learned over the years that obviously I didn't know then.

It was as though you embraced painting for the first time, despite the fact that you'd been working as a painter rather than as a sculptor or a video artist. Perhaps the subject matter that you were dealing with might have been better expressed through other mediums at those early stages.
– In fact, it was just that I went through art college as a painter and that's what I happened to do. It is also the most direct way of making a mark on a piece of paper or canvas, a straightforward expression of human activity. But yes, I could, I suppose, equally well have been using other media, but in those days maybe it didn't occur to me, maybe I couldn't afford to use other mediums.

Do you think your development, at the beginning of the 80s, was also to do with a recognition that you could reveal yourself a bit, that you could maybe become vulnerable through your work?

Latter Day Church of the Bleeding Heart, *1993, oil on wood, 164 x 68cm*

– Yes, exactly, it marked a watershed in my own personal development as well, it was a coming together of all sorts of things. And yes, it was also to do with laying myself open and making myself more vulnerable.

Traditionally political art, or historical painting, are usually an expression of the 'public', an interest in conveying very specific ideological positions; whereas for you, the intersection with the political and historical seems to have been a very personal one.
– Yes, I don't deny that. It was, yes.

After that, you began accepting particular commissions?
– Well, not immediately after that, there were really only two there's the mining one 1989-90, and after that there's the Gulf one. I had become interested in the notion of war and countries at war through the Falklands War, and realising that having been in a state of peace for however many years throughout my life was actually quite unusual for many people throughout the world. It has become quite important to me to address this in some way, it started creeping into my work with topics related to Third World countries. In particular I focused on Nicaragua as a place to go. I was fed up with the pontificating from afar about what's going on in these places and making comments about it, but without any firsthand experience. So I hatched the idea of going to a country at war for a period of research, just to see what came of it, and if I could make some work out of it, then so much the better.

Nicaragua was a place that interested me politically. It seemed obviously one of these proxy wars that was waged indirectly with the support of the US and the Soviet Union; and also it was a place that was worthy of attention because there seemed to be some sort of historical experiment going on there which was interesting. So I thought I'd go and see what I found, and that resulted in a series of paintings entitled *Bee-keeping in the War Zone*, which was at the Angela Flowers Gallery in 1987.

Was this the first time you crossed the boundary of security?
– Yes, it was.

Were you taking to that experience, an existing visual language, or was it only your subject matter that was being altered ?
– It didn't radically alter my approach, but I think it perhaps expanded the language and the ways I was using paint.

You began to use collage. Or had you done it before?
– It had come into things before, but it became much more of a feature of my work, and also the idea, the titles and writing on the paintings, which featured very heavily. The collage and so on is to do with bringing back actual objects, items, newspapers, bills, money and so on, which had been part of the experience of being there. I also began to use devices like the use of my own shadow coming into paintings, to get across the idea that this was very much my view of the situation, a subjective view.

You frequently seem to comment on the impossibility of encapsulating experiences through your art, so there's always a frustration. Like your earlier adoption of irony in place of theory.

– There's an undermining of myself in a way, in that I don't necessarily believe what I'm saying about something. I have a voice that says, 'Well, look, this is arguable, but this is what I think about it,' rather than the didacticism of some political work. I hate being preached at, I think it probably makes more enemies than people it wins over.

Is it true that your paintings, often viewed as political and interventionist, are not about what's out there, they're about you?

– Yes, I think there is obviously a very marked element of the personal about them, but I hope that doesn't completely obscure some of the comments, or commentary, that I'm seeking to introduce. Detractors might well say that, yes, but the fact that I'm doing it in the first place, going, dealing with that subject matter itself in the first place, I think that marks it out.

After the Nicaraguan series, I thought, 'Well, what next?' It seemed to me that I'd been halfway round the world to get excited and involved in something that was going on, that really had very little, in a direct way, to do with myself. Whilst, on the other hand, along with most other people on the British mainland, I felt baffled, bemused and I really ignored what was going on in the north of Ireland for the last 20 years, and this was going on on my doorstep.

I do have a family connection as well with that part of the world, and I suddenly became interested to try and understand it, to try to address it. So I organised a trip there and stayed with relatives. There was a period of research, talking to a lot of people, just making my way around, taking photographs, talking to Sinn Fein, going on patrol with the UDR (Ulster Defence Regiment), and immersing myself as much as possible; but really I think just trying to listen and understand what people were saying, and then filter that afterwards through into my work again.

The research period is very important. Do you see that as something essential to all your projects?

– All the projects, yes. There's also a lot of work that I do that isn't specifically about projects, but it's an intense period of absorption. It's like being a journalist, I suppose, except that I'm not writing stories, I'm making art.

Does the organisation of compositions, happen after the research is digested, without reference to it?

– No, I refer to it. When I've gone home and I'm thinking about it, I'm sifting through the material that I've gathered, and ideas begin to emerge and I just write down notes and so on, and then things start to come together.

Have you come to a conclusion before you start painting, or is the painting part of that process of understanding?

– It's usually attempting to distil an idea, that I have, about something that I've come across.

I said 'conclusion' because you said that you were interested in the different sides of an argument. In the paintings, not that they're totally directed, but you have come to a conclusion about where you stand vis-à-vis *the material. Do you start off without that conclusion, or do you delay the emergence of it.*

– I would definitely start off with preconceptions, which might be confirmed or undermined, but I would like to think, whatever my preconceptions were, that they're somehow modified by the actual experience – because otherwise what would be the point of doing it? And often there are things you just don't know about, that you couldn't possibly have considered without actually going there and finding out and talking to people and discovering things yourself.

The work on the miners' project was rather different, as you started to look at the whole concept of disruption, war and antagonisms in an even more political way?

– You're thinking about the miners' strike and running down the industry and all that. I think that was implicit rather than obvious. I wasn't taking that head on. The colliery that I went to, Ollerton, is actually where the UDM (Union of Democratic Mineworkers) started out, so in the history of the struggle they were the villains. It was interesting talking to them about it, but that really wasn't what was high on my agenda. It was an unknown world to me, a world that everyone takes for granted and the everyday life of people who went underground to get the coal is something that really most people, not involved in it, have no conception of. At first I was a bit worried about actually going underground, I'm a bit claustrophobic, and I'd recently given up taking the Underground in London. I must say I felt safer going down a coalmine. Actually I found it fascinating; I think it was partly some childhood fascination with tunnels.

Here there was another shift, to an interest in the heroism of everyday life, moving away from the critique or the ironic.

– I think there was something particular to that project that demanded a more classical approach, I suppose, partly just because of my unfamiliarity with just what it's like being underground. I'd hate to have to do it every day, but the people who do it are proud to do it, and fight tooth and nail to be able to retain the right to do it. But it's the strangeness of it, of something which has been completely fundamental to all our lives.

Going underground is like trying to find those experiences that are totally alien to you, even when you're back in England.

– Well, that's right, and in a sense it's a front line as well, literally that cutting machine is just slicing through layers of the earth's crust, and it's dangerous.

How much do you produce your work for specific audiences, or how much is the work to do with trying to understand the experiences yourself?

– I think it's probably unfortunate, but it's a fact of life, that where I've taken on a commission it does have some effect on my work. They're commissioning me on the basis of what they know about my work, and so obviously I'm going to produce the kind of thing that seems to me suitable and apt. But obviously, at the same time I have this sense of someone looking over my shoulder, which makes me a bit uncomfortable. So maybe it changes a bit. But otherwise, if it's just a project of my own, I just do exactly what I want. I mean, it's important to me, yes, how people feel about what I've done, and whether I feel work is successful or not, and I do gauge that on what people say. Obviously not doing things to please or to satisfy, but things that I feel will work.

Being the War Artist in the Gulf, this relationship must have always been far more testing and dynamic?

– Well, I knew that it was going to come under an enormous amount of public scrutiny, and also there was the wording of the contract; that I was to record the activities, I think it went, 'of the British and Allied Forces during the Gulf War', which, frankly, was not really what interested me. But I felt somehow that some of the work that I did, probably I did in a way to fulfil that contract. In the end the work that they actually bought from what I'd produced, and I produced over 50 paintings, was one that I'd just done because I wanted to. The *Mickey Mouse at the Front* painting was one where I wasn't really bearing in mind what the Artistic Records Committee might have wanted. I was very pleased with their choice, and I think it's quite a bold choice, and it raised a lot of eyebrows and caused a certain amount of controversy. But I think it somehow vindicates my approach. I mean, if someone's commissioning you, they're commissioning you for who you are and the work they know you've produced in the past, not because they want to somehow prescribe what it is you produce.

You had already confronted similar issues in your early work. Was this experience fundamentally a different one?

– Yes, it was, in that I'd never been set down in a full-scale war situation. You know, Northern Ireland and Nicaragua are completely different kinds of conflict. The world hadn't seen such a massive deployment of military hardware since the end of the Second World War, so that in itself was extraordinary. But the main thing, I think, was this feeling of being completely dependent, which I found very uncomfortable. They were my lifeline. There was this feeling of being unable to detach myself from it. I wouldn't do that again under the same circumstances. It's not that I wouldn't go to a situation like that, but I wouldn't lay myself open, or make myself so dependent on that back up.

There was a lot of analysis in those works. It appeared to me, as a spectator, that the works were trying to bring together a lot of very complicated things that were not obviously to do just with what you had experienced, as opposed to the other projects where you talk about the research period coming first. It was almost as though there was the experience and then there was the research.

– It was, yes. I was there for under five weeks, and it was extremely intense. I was bundled around from one place to another, between the Army, the Navy and the Air Force, it was extremely confusing, and it was very difficult to make any sense at the time of what it was I was seeing or what was happening. Indeed, information was often quite hard to come by. Particularly, for instance, when I was at sea, there was no information coming at all and I felt very frustrated, and that was when the actual ground war was happening. Also there were occasions when I felt much more physically threatened than I've ever felt anywhere else. The experience of going through gas alerts and so on is not something I particularly want to repeat. So it was a very dense experience, that probably took quite a bit of unravelling to analyse subsequently. So I suppose it's quite a perceptive point, the difference you observed in that work to previous projects.

Did you feel that the changing relationship between your work and the experiential and analytical has shifted any more since the Gulf War paintings?

– I wouldn't say in any obvious way. The whole thing now seems like an extraordinary dream. Actually being there was so remote from any other reality that I've had before or since, that it doesn't really relate to anything else, and whatever bearing that has had subsequently, I think would probably need a psychologist to unravel.

Your exhibition at the Riverside Studios in 1994, dealt primarily with the idea of religious fundamentalism, and references to German expressionism, in the 20s and 30s, seem far more apparent. You are no longer an observer, you're involved.

– Maybe that reflects what I have been feeling about what is happening at the moment. The allusions in that work are to the way I've seen the world going in the last few years, particularly since the breakdown of the Eastern bloc. Things like Bosnia going on very close to home, and our capacity to largely ignore what's happening there, and other things like, say, the re-emergence of fascism or fundamentalism, all those extremes I do feel threatened by, and I think the world is threatened by.

Previously, you seem to be trying to understand the reasons for conflict, now you seem to have decided that maybe one can't.

– Well, maybe I'm trying to deal with topics that I think brook no reason, the aspects of human behaviour that are not open to reason or argument. There's a much more atavistic process at work, and that is what I find disturbing. That's why, some of the works in that show are called *Dark Ages*. We like to think of ourselves as civilised and that the Dark Ages were something way back in history, but perhaps we flatter ourselves and civilised values are just a thin veneer that's easily peeled back.

Certain audiences could look at the Dark Ages *works, and see them as commenting on the world of unreason, beyond the constraints of our notion of civilisation. Is that true, or were you talking about worlds quite close to home?*
– That's what I was saying, that it could be close to home. I think, given the right circumstances. I mean, it harks back to the Falklands War and suddenly finding ourselves at war, and thinking that this had been unthinkable, but yet there it was happening. It is easy to condemn from a distance, but under the right circumstances you could indeed be guilty perhaps of the things that you are condemning others for. However, there are things in this show that I do take issue with, and ought to be argued with. It is an argument with the metaphysical ideas of religion, in the form of atrocity or intolerance, based on arguments that you cannot really discuss or argue with because there's no arguing with God.

It seems to make you very angry.
– The more I think about it, the more angry it does make me. I mean, there's much about religions and religious doctrines that interests me and that is good, but the other side of that coin is intolerance and extremes of hatred. And there's the philosophical aspects as well, the exclusiveness of an idea of truth, that cannot be modified. There are ideas which have been laid down in tablets of stone, millennia ago, that we cannot argue with.

There's been a lot of interest recently in the idea that you can construct the notion of national identity, through art in particular. Do you believe there is Britishness in art?
– I think there is. There are British characteristics which, well, even though a lot of the artists who are recognised as British often have come from other backgrounds, but yes, there is a sort of Britishness. I mean, when you think about Sutherland or Nash or Hitchins or Hodgkin, there are qualities there, I don't know that I'd like to describe them, that fit within one's understanding of what British art is. And yet there are lots of people who break out. But for myself, I don't know. There's a lot about me, my personality and the person I am, which is obviously British, but I'm not sure how that manifests itself in the work, which I think is a bit uncharacteristic. I don't know if you'd agree.

I think that when you start to define too closely the idea of a visual language growing from the specifics of a nation, it can be quite dangerous: it can get back to the essential problem in Bosnia. Where does commitment and positioning within a humanistic morality fit with the idea of expressing the specifics of nation?
– But Britishness, don't you think, is inevitably tied up with a landscape tradition.

I suppose traditionally that's how people view work like that of Long or Goldsworthy, as part a relationship with nature.
– But not given to histrionics or passion. It's not something you'd describe as characteristic of British art.

I suppose the expectations are of the commentator, who deals with things in a quieter way. That's where I feel you are fighting against those definitions, that your work has been a transgression of the expected characteristics of Britishness.
– I think it's partly to do with shrugging off my upbringing. In fact, the decision to become an artist, a painter, is not something that my parents would in any way have expected from me, because it's quite alien to them. I don't come from an artistic or particularly cultured background of any kind. It was at the age of 15 or something like that I decided I wanted to go to art school, at the time it was a bit of an act of rebellion. And I think ever since I've been trying to escape from my background and upbringing, and trying to redefine myself.

Is there a big project under way?
– Well, I don't know. I was quite interested in doing another project, which is going to Cuba while it still exists.

You have always seemed to explore the point where the individual intersects with the ideological.
– Yes, and history, and how do you make paintings about that, but that's where the challenge continually is. I mean, you have this information that interests you, it's not traditionally part of what painting is about – it might be part of what writing novels or making films is about – and that's part of the thrill.

Do you have to be a painter? Do you think that part of it is something you could be doing as a novelist, as a film maker?
– I could be, but I can't. I tried writing a novel once, and it was crap and it was very difficult. The thing about painting is that I love doing it. It's so direct, you can get on with it by yourself. If you're in a play or something, you need other actors.

So where do you place the set of works in The Struggle for the Control of the Television Station*? There are themes and elements that seem to grow out of the Gulf paintings.*
– There are references to images, like the childhood Mickey Mouse, but the notion behind the title of that show and that central piece was the television station as an object of desire for our times. The sort of thing exemplified in a political way, that now, if you're staging a coup, you don't go for the seat of government, you go and take over the television station. If you've got hold of that, it suggests that you've got your hold on a seat of power. Also, not just by violent means, but it alludes to, for instance, Berlusconi in Italy, that here's a media magnate who was running the country. The television station, a seat of communication, is a centre of control in all ways, both by direct

Mickey Mouse at the Front, *1991, oil on canvas;* PAGE 96: The Struggle for the Control of the Television Station, *1992, oil on canvas, 330 x 407cm*

propaganda but also through much more subtle means, just the way we think about things and see things. TV is a world of glamour that people aspire to, and also that people will suffer the most outrageous humiliation just to be seen on television. So it works on all levels, really, and some of the paintings, not all of them, in this show were about that phenomenon.

Do you feel quite isolated within the British art world, or do you see yourself as working within a set of shared concerns?
– I suppose in the 80s maybe I could have fitted in. Well, that re-emergence of figurative painting, and the Glasgow thing, I mean, I'm not from that background, but I did from time to time get lumped in with that. But otherwise, no.

But you also seem to be using more and more obvious symbolic language; the skeletal images, the skulls.
– I was deliberately trying to just get into that and use allegory in that way.

So the painting itself has a different relationship to experience.
– Yes, it does, in that it's more distilled into allegorical themes and topics. It's more to do with a instinctive response, to measure a kind of *Zeitgeist*, to just put my finger on the pulse in a very unspecific way.

They're very bleak paintings, aren't they, and then, if one goes on to look at the recent show at the Riverside, there does seem to be a sense in which you're becoming far more pessimistic.
– If you substitute 'angry' for 'pessimistic', I think maybe that's a clearer image. There's something more positive about anger.

The struggle to grasp what it is you're doing doesn't seem quite there any more. The struggle seems to be to grasp the solutions.
– Yes. Well, maybe I'm less content with taking certain attitudes. It's not that I'm not seeking so hard to understand, it's that perhaps I just want to be a bit more rhetorical now.

Certain elements have recurred throughout many of the projects you've been involved in, for over a decade. For instance, the shopping trolley, which seems to have been around for a while.
– That first appeared, I think it was about 1985, maybe, when I saw a newspaper photograph after the riots at the Broadwater Farm in London. There's a photograph of a shopping trolley that's loaded with missiles of various kinds by the crowd. What fascinated me was that this vehicle that we normally go around a supermarket with and fill with consumer goods, had been turned into a weapon of war and aggression, as a sort of sad comment on our society. And then it cropped up in many guises, just obviously as a symbol of the age of the consumer. It came into its own in Kuwait City, when I was wandering around the front after

the Iraqis had left, and by the sea there was a shopping trolley loaded with rocket-propelled grenades.

A visual resonance
– It was like something out of a painting I'd already done. It was one of those uncanny images that just demanded to be used.

One of the things about the way in which you use collage seems to be that the elements appear to me to be manifestations of very specific ideologies. Often there's a lot of money, or in the Irish series, there are pages from a very pernicious Loyalist magazine and things like that.
– Whether it's printed matter, or indeed actual objects in some cases, there are things that often I have come across that seem relevant. I mean, just on a purely technical, aesthetic level, I enjoy playing around with the surface of the painting and what works within an illusionary space and what remains there on the surface of the canvas; trying to knock something on the surface back into the field of painting.

Is the Riverside exhibition the first to include a self-portrait?
– Ah, no, no, there have been many others, actually. There's one I did in the Gulf War, in a gas mask.

Well, a self-portrait in a gas mask is slightly ambiguous.
– Yes, I know. But maybe this is a more graphic self-portrait. There was also one in the Nicaraguan series, the portrait of the artist pretending to be a guerrilla.

In disguise.
– The cultural guerrilla.

So are you in disguise in this one, even though you're standing naked, with your heart in your hand?
– Well, they're all wry comments about myself, the bleeding heart liberal or the petrified war artist in the back of a Land Rover in a gas mask. There was also one, *Portrait of the artist as a small boy in Northern Ireland*, me on holiday.

And the idea of the revelation of self in this self-portrait, is still ironic, that you're suddenly without any costume or disguise.
– Yes, it is ironic, but it's also serious, exposing myself in all senses of the word.

Oriana Baddeley is Principal Lecturer in the History of Art and Design at Camberwell College of Arts and co-author, with Valerie Fraser, of Drawing Line: Art and Cultural Identity in Contemporary Latin America, Verso, 1989. *She is currently working on a book on Mexican art and is compiling an anthology of theoretical writings on art and multiculturalism.*